MARKETING MIXOLOGY

Ambi Parameswaran is a consultant, coach and founder of brand-building.com, a brand advisory. Over the last forty-five years, he has been involved in building brands, as a marketer, as a marketing communications professional and, over the last ten years, as an independent brand coach.

A large part of Ambi's career was spent in building FCB Ulka into one of the top three ad agency groups in India. He is a much demanded keynote speaker and has worked with more than a hundred brands/companies, including Tata Motors, Wipro, ICICI Bank, Zee TV, TCS, Thermax, ITC, LIC, J&J, Pepsico, Amul, Tropicana, Abbott, Sun Pharma, Digene, Santoor, Sundrop and many more.

His columns appear regularly in business publications like *Business Standard*, *Hindustan Times*, *Economic Times*, etc. He is a guest faculty member at IIM Ahmedabad, IIM Calcutta and is an adjunct professor of marketing at SPJIMR, Mumbai. He is also a distinguished alumnus awardee from both IIT Madras and IIM Calcutta, an AMP graduate from Harvard Business School, holds a PhD in management from Mumbai University and is a CFI-certified CEO coach.

Ambi is a strong proponent of the philosophy of lifelong learning and believes that reading, writing, teaching and coaching keeps him mentally agile. He is the author of eleven books on branding, marketing, advertising and self-development.

He can be reached at ambimgp@brand-building.com or you can follow him on LinkedIn (@AmbiParameswaran) and on X/Twitter (@ambimgp).

Marketing Mixology – Advance Praise

'*Marketing Mixology* by Ambi Parameswaran is a must-read for anyone seeking a practical, no-nonsense guide to marketing success. It brilliantly distills complex concepts into four essential skills, backed by real-world insights from top CMOs. Whether you're a novice or a seasoned marketer, this book is your roadmap to mastering marketing.'

—Kunal Bahl, co-founder, Titan Capital and Snapdeal

'In this lovely book, Ambi Parameswaran stirs up a delightful cocktail of marketing wisdom. Practical, enjoyable and thought-provoking, Ambi's deep insights and invaluable advice are drawn from an illustrious career spanning five decades. A sparkling read!'

—Harish Bhat, bestselling author and
former brand custodian, Tata Sons

'Instead of getting tipsy on zany new marketing, try Ambi's classic wine. My favourite was the chapter on negotiating and selling.'

—Sudhir Sitapati, CEO and MD, Godrej

'Reading this book feels like you are chatting with your favourite marketing guru on anything and everything you need to know about marketing. Written with a light humorous touch, seeded with gems of insight from industry practitioners, it provides an excellent foundation for anyone keen to build a brand … anecdotes and cartoons help the narrative sparkle. Here's a book that you'll keep coming back to.'

—Jessie Paul, marketing expert

'*Marketing Mixology* is a unique, refreshing and stimulating cocktail of concepts and case studies with liberal splashes of wisdom from successful practitioners.'

—Rama Bijapurkar, author of *Lilliput Land* and
We are Like that Only

'With *Marketing Mixology*, Ambi Parameswaran has crafted the ultimate primer for modern marketers. In a world cluttered with jargon, this book offers clarity on the fundamental marketing skills that truly matter. Parameswaran distills decades of experience into an accessible guide that every aspiring marketer, entrepreneur, and business leader should read. If you've ever wished for a marketing mentor who could guide you through the essentials with ease and clarity, *Marketing Mixology* is the book you need.'

—K. Ganesh, serial entrepreneur, promoter and author of *Mastering Disruption: A Practical Guide to New-Age Business Models*

'Ambi's deep expertise and engaging storytelling make the book a must-read for those who want to master marketing. A brilliant addition to every marketer's bookshelf!'

—Farooq Adam, founder, Fynd

'*Marketing Mixology* is a masterclass in modern marketing, blending decades of experience, real-world insights, and practical frameworks into a compelling and easy-to-digest guide. Ambi Parameswaran has distilled the essence of what it takes to succeed as a marketer—understanding consumers deeply, building brands with purpose, mastering the art of selling and negotiation, and communicating with clarity and impact. This book is an invaluable companion. Ambi's storytelling and hands-on wisdom make it an engaging read that leaves you not just informed, but inspired.'

—Harshil Karia,
founder, Schbang and co-founder, Level Supermind

'A very different take on marketing—consumer-centric, with practical frameworks and ideas to become better at the craft.'

—Radhika Gupta, MD and CEO, Edelweiss Mutual Fund

AMBI PARAMESWARAN

MARKETING MIXOLOGY

FOUR ESSENTIAL INGREDIENTS FOR MARKETING SUCCESS

WESTLAND
BUSINESS

WESTLAND
BUSINESS

Published by Westland Business, an imprint of Westland Books, a division of Nasadiya Technologies Private Limited, in 2025

No. 269/2B, First Floor, 'Irai Arul', Vimalraj Street, Nethaji Nagar, Alapakkam Main Road, Maduravoyal, Chennai 600095

Westland, the Westland logo, Westland Business and the Westland Business logo are the trademarks of Nasadiya Technologies Private Limited, or its affiliates.

ISBN: 9789360453220

10 9 8 7 6 5 4 3

Typeset by Mukul

Printed at Thomson Press (India) Ltd

To all my students, who continue to inspire me to keep learning

Contents

The Four Essential Marketing Skills

'How can I get a quick refresher on marketing?'

'Can you tell me how I can get a job in marketing?'

'Does an entrepreneur who is busy running his company really need to know all this marketing funda?'

'Can you give me a crash course on marketing that will prepare me for the job interview?'

'If I want to be successful in marketing, what are the core skills I should have?'

I have been asked these questions and more over the last forty-five years of my career in marketing, advertising and coaching. When I sat down to interview twenty-five chief marketing officers (CMOs) from large and mid-sized companies across the world in 2021–2022, these questions echoed in my mind. Specifically, I couldn't help but think about how their learnings as they climbed up the marketing ladder, coupled with my own experience, could make for an interesting book on practical marketing skills.

(You can access all the twenty-five interviews on the *ET BrandEquity* YouTube channel via the QR code. I have included a few quotes from those conversations in the course of the book. Please note that these CMOs may be in different roles or organisations when this book reaches you, but their words will always be of value.)

How does one learn about marketing? I can suggest many books for you to read, including highly venerated textbooks that run well over 400 pages. I have co-authored one of the most widely used books on strategic brand management myself.

If you belong to the TL;DR crowd (too long; didn't read), then you might shrug and say, 'Well, I don't have the time for this.' Or you may be in the camp that has read those big books, but need a quick refresher instead of leafing through those tomes again. In any case, this book is for you if you want a quick overview of the essential skills for marketing. It's easy to read and full of relevant examples, and I have provided a snapshot of what I believe are four essential skills for marketing success. This is a book that can give you many useful tips, maybe even help you answer a few questions during an interview!

What is the one thing that separates a marketing executive from all the others in the company? All of them have to be able to handle numbers. All of them have to get along with their colleagues. All of them have to have analytical skills. All of them have to have basic levels of written and oral communication skills. What more?

This is where *Marketing Mixology* can help. It goes beyond the typical 'marketing mix' that business school students mouth mechanically, i.e., the four Ps of marketing: price, product, place and promotion (in recent times a few more Ps have been added: people, processes, packaging). When I talk of *Marketing Mixology*, I am going to go beyond the typical 'marketing mix' definition. Just like a great cocktail is made through mixology, a successful marketing career can be built on the basis of what you can rapidly glean from this handy book. Irrespective of your choice of drinks, you can enjoy this book and get to a new high in your career or your business.

What really is the key to success in a marketing career?

Undoubtedly, marketing starts with the ability to understand consumers or customers. And so, **understanding consumers** will be the first essential skill we will explore in this book. All the twenty-five CMOs, without exception, reiterated that they spend time talking to customers, get involved with consumer research and more. Peter Drucker, a management guru without parallel, said, 'The only purpose of a corporation is to create and retain a customer.' You cannot create a customer if you don't know them. All marketing begins with a deep dive into consumer beliefs, attitudes and behaviour.

> 'I meet thirty to fifty clients myself within the first few weeks of joining any job, even if there is no research study going on. This is the rigour I still employ.'
>
> *—Deepali Naair, Director of Marketing (India/South Asia), IBM*

Once we understand where the consumer is coming from, we then get into the task of crafting a marketing/brand plan. The second essential skill we will explore is that of **brand building**. It was marketing guru Philip Kotler who gave this equation: 'Marketing = Branding.' There is no marketing without branding. Brands are today ubiquitous. The local kirana merchant knows the brands he stocks. He knows some brands have a consumer 'pull' while many need his 'push' support.

How do you build brands? Can you just put a name on a product and expect it to become a brand? In the second chapter, you will discover a simple five-step process of brand building that I call the Brand Building Pentagon (BBP). By following these five steps, you can build a strong brand if you are starting from scratch. If you already have a brand that you want to take to the next level, BBP will point you in the right direction with the right questions. Branding is also a topic that came up in my discussions with the

CMOs. All of them are proud of the brands they handle and are acutely aware of how important it is to manage a brand so that its equity is protected and enhanced.

What else should a marketing executive know? What sets them apart from the others in the company?

A marketing executive is always selling. They are selling their ideas inside the company. They are selling their brand outside as well, to retailers and customers. So the third essential skill we will explore will be **selling and negotiation**. Negotiation is not of interest solely to folks in marketing—we are all negotiating all the time. When you discuss with your daughter about the toy she will get for her birthday, that's negotiation. You probably negotiated your pay package when you joined a new company. In the third chapter, you will discover the importance of doing your homework, understanding the other side and how to go beyond mere give-and-take, which is how most people view negotiation.

When it comes to selling, it may seem simple: just sell what you have. But even in this scenario, you have to understand the process of selling. How to open a discussion. How to build buyer interest. How to take it to the final order. In this chapter, you will discover the SPANCO model of selling, something that is essential for business-to-business (B2B) enterprises.

The fourth essential skill for success in marketing is the ability to communicate well.

If you are in marketing, you have to be good at communication—written, oral, one-on-one, one-to-many. After all, marketing requires one to be good at convincing and storytelling. The fourth chapter in this book will take you into key aspects of **communication skills**. Starting from simple one-on-one communication, we will explore aspects of marketing communication that involve digital media and offline media like TV and print. The fundamentals of communication do not change even if the media changes. You have to tell your consumer something in a way that they will be interested in reading or watching. That may sound simple, but after seeing hundreds of ads on all media, we know that not all brands manage to get this right. This chapter will lay down some simple steps for you to ensure that you do better when it comes to communicating with your target segments: a single shopkeeper, your sales team or your end consumer.

> 'You need to develop the pulse for the consumer mindset. Because all things you do, whether it is brand communication, execution or setting up an offline strategy, requires you to understand the mindset.'
>
> *—Siddhesh Joglekar, VP, Marketing, BYJU's*

In this book, you will take a deep dive into these four essential skills. But you may ask, is that all? Not really. To be successful in marketing, you do need several more skills. I will outline some of them in the last chapter.

Now, let's get ready to learn about the essential skills that will up your marketing quotient. I have explained them in simple, everyday terms. Keep a pen handy. And … happy journey into *Marketing Mixology*!

1

The Deep Dive: Understanding Consumers

The aim of marketing is to know and understand the customer so well that the product or service fits him and sells itself.

—Peter Drucker

I was sitting with a client from Kathmandu who had approached me to help them with their marketing strategy. My first question to them was, 'Do you know who your customers are?'

They were a little taken aback. They were clocking in sales of over ₹10 crore per month, so there was no shortage of customers buying their product. 'Of course we know who our customers are!' they said.

'Okay, then tell me about them,' I replied.

'We make shoes. They are comfortable and offer great value for money. So our customers are middle-income people who do not want to stretch their budget too much.'

'That's fine. But who are they? Where do they live? Why are they selecting your brand and not any one of the other hundred brands in the market?' I asked.

'Well, we launched our product in two states—UP and Bihar. We supply to the wholesalers in those markets. They seem to be happy with our product. They tell us that our products are sold in smaller towns.'

'Have you met the person who is buying your shoes? Have you spoken with them?'

'No, we are just too busy making shoes. We don't have the time to go and meet customers. Do you think that will help us?' they asked.

In response, I narrated a story that I had heard about India's biggest automotive brand. Maruti Suzuki, when it was undergoing a transformation journey in the 2000s, insisted that every supervisor across all departments spend at least a day in the year meeting customers and selling to them. They called this initiative 'Each One Sell One'. It brought about a great sense of realisation of consumer perceptions across the length and breadth of the company.

The next hour with my client was spent discussing how it is important for their company to know more about the end customer of their products. After all, understanding customers is the primary job of someone in marketing.

Every industry has its own little guidelines. Most hotels insist that their general managers (GM) spend some time mingling with their guests to get first-hand consumer feedback. As a designer friend who works with hotels pointed out to me, you can make out the leadership quality of a GM the moment you walk into the lobby of a five-star hotel.

Many consumer product companies insist that their marketing teams spend at least five days a month carrying out dealer visits; some even expect the marketing team to visit the homes of their typical customer.

Unfortunately, many companies are stuck in what may be product-first thinking. In this mode, companies obsess over their product, paying scant regard to where the consumer is coming from. More sensitive business leaders manage to bridge the gap by bringing in a stronger consumer-first orientation. Why is that important? How is that going to help us design better products and services? And what are the ways of learning more about consumers?

Who Is the Consumer?

In this chapter, we will use the terms 'consumers' and 'customers' interchangeably. Often, the term 'consumers' is used in business-to-customer (B2C) marketing, while 'customers' (or 'clients') is more common in B2B marketing.

Depending on the product category, consumers are all around you. If you are working on a product, your mom or your friends could be potential consumers. When developing a product like a pain-relief balm, you can get useful information from your domestic helpers and even your cab driver. If you want to understand why a consumer buys a premium mobile phone, you may want to speak with a friend who buys a fancy new handset every year.

But how does one speak to consumers? There is no manual that will tell you what to do. I prefer talking to consumers just as you would talk to a friend. Keep the conversation informal without making the respondent overly conscious about what they are saying. If they become self-conscious, they may try to guess the answer you are looking for. And that will give you what is called GIGO data—garbage in, garbage out.

Even before you start having these conversations, develop a set of questions that will give you relevant information. While the order of the questions needn't be set in stone, having a set of questions will ensure you get all your data. For example, when working on a sugar substitute, these were some of the questions my associates and I asked our friends:

- Do you use sugar for your daily tea?
- Are you aware of the calories contained in a spoonful of sugar?
- Would you call yourself calorie-conscious?
- Have you used a sugar substitute before?
- What benefits do you expect from a sugar substitute?
- What are the cons of using a sugar substitute?

With just a handful of simple questions, we got the ball rolling and then thought of more as the discussion progressed.

Apart from the customers themselves, retailers too can be great sources of information. You can speak with them informally to get their views on why consumers buy a product/brand and what may be holding them back. It may also be important for you to find out the role played by the retailer in the brand choice.

Yet another variant of this direct form of questioning is to do an observation study. Quietly stand at a retail counter and watch the interactions between the retailer and customers for an hour or more (after informing the retailer, of course).

As mentioned earlier, many consumer marketing companies have now mandated that all marketing executives have to spend one day a month carrying out 'home visits'. Sometimes, members of product development teams are also called to join these expeditions. Home visits help someone who may not know how the 'average' consumer lives gain some first-hand experience. However, the consumer may 'dress up' their home. While visiting a few lower-income homes for a project, we noticed that a few households prominently displayed empty cartons of Dove, a premium soap. The soap in the soap dish was not Dove, but the housewife had 'dressed up' her home to indicate that they were very brand-conscious. In yet another series of home visits we did in north India in the 2000s, we requested the housewife to show us the refrigerator. Inside, we only saw milk, curd and vegetables; most homes did not store cooked food in the refrigerator. This observation was validated through further research and was used in the development of marketing campaigns (Whirlpool's 'Ice Baby' television spot was a big hit).

While working on B2B brands, you will need to adapt a consumer immersion process. You may want to speak with buyers of the service, opinion leaders and subject matter experts. Recently, while doing a study for an email solutions company, I reached out to the chief technology officers (CTOs) of five companies to have an informal chat with them on how their company decided on their email solutions provider. I had a set of questions that I modified as I completed each interview. While the users of email were the employees of the company, the decision regarding the email service was in the hands of the CTOs.

There are, however, a few risks in this kind of research. Your company may be headquartered in Delhi or Mumbai. You may end up doing mere dipstick research in those cities alone—what happens outside the metro cities may be very different. One must be cautious not to apply metro city findings to the rest of India. Dipstick research is not a replacement for in-depth research done by a neutral third-party research agency. However, dipstick surveys do help in being able to better define what the consumer research project will need to explore. Ideally, you should engage a third-party consumer research agency *after* you have done your own little immersion.

If you are in marketing, you have to be able to make casual conversations with a shopkeeper or a customer. Just the other day, I was at a chemist's shop. I noticed a middle-aged man buying two packs of Electral, an oral rehydration salt. Curious, I politely asked him, 'Sir, are you unwell? Why are you buying two packs of Electral?'

The person wanted to know why I asked. When I clarified that I am associated with the company that makes Electral, he was happy to speak: 'No, no, sir I am perfectly healthy. I am an electrician. I feel tired while working through the day. Electral is great to keep me going. I start the day by buying two packs of it.'

The answer surprised me. Obviously, he was not the typical customer of Electral, yet he was a far more regular consumer than a patient. There are a few lessons to take away from this. One, if you want to be in marketing you should be ready to speak with strangers and also be ready to be told to get lost. Second, you cannot make assumptions about why they are buying or not buying a brand. Speaking to retailers too is something you should master if you want to get insights from them.

As we speak to consumers, we will find out that not all of them buy the same products in the same way. What are the methods of analysing how they go about buying a product?

How Do Consumers Buy?

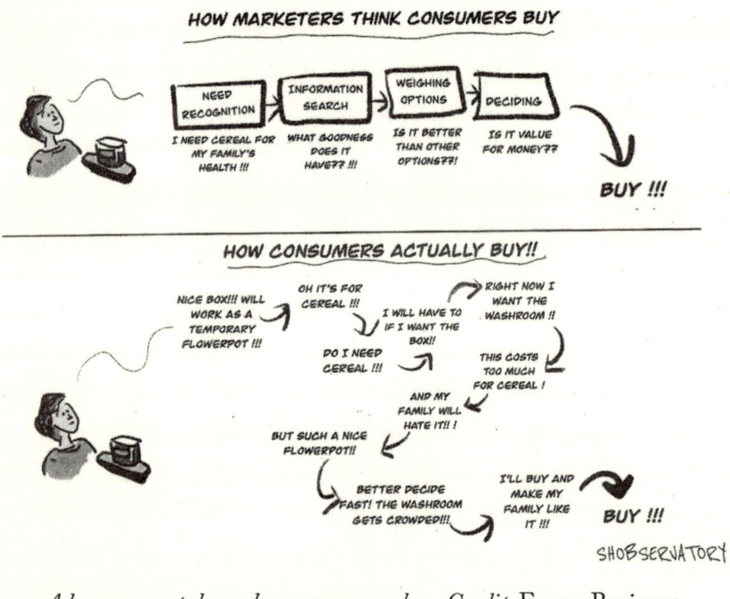

A humourous take on how consumers buy. Credit: Funny Business, *Shobha Prasad*

Most of the time, consumers do not buy without thinking. They often go through a process of decision-making: recognition of need, search for alternatives, evaluation of alternatives, the act of purchase, usage of the product and post-usage reaction. But do all of us recognise needs the same way? An air conditioner is a basic need for someone. For someone else, a ceiling fan may be a luxury.

What determines this? There are two types of influences that work on our decision-making: environmental influences and individual differences.

We are a product of our environment. The society we live in, our family, our upbringing—these are **environmental influences**. We are all shaped by society, and much of what we consume and how we consume is shaped by our family and our upbringing. In my book *Nawabs, Nudes, Noodles—India Through 50 Years of Advertising*, I have explored the way sociocultural trends have been reflected in the advertising we have seen in India over the last fifty years. Some decades ago, it was only the man of the household who did all the shopping for the home, which included buying groceries. This seems incredible, but it is true that even now, in some parts of rural India, it is the man who does the grocery shopping. Factors such as the penetration of electricity, television, better access to big cities through roads and now the internet and smartphones have changed our buying behaviour. When you want to buy a new phone or are looking for a plumber, you search the internet for instant suggestions instead of depending on your neighbours' recommendations.

If the environment shapes our buying behaviour, we cannot ignore that no two consumers are alike. Each consumer has **individual differences** that come into play. Differences include the money we have in the wallet or our disposable income. Differences could also arise due to our education, occupation or where we live. Our buying behaviour is also shaped by our distinct personalities. Some of us are extroverts and some of us are introverts. Some of us want to flaunt our wealth, some want to hide it. Our personality shapes all things we do, from how we talk and dress to how we shop.

In a vast country like India, there is a need to see how we can segment and analyse consumers. Variables like geography (UP/Bihar/Tamil Nadu) and monthly household income (MHI) are commonly used. We also use socio-economic classification (SEC) to segment consumers. Here, we look at data about the household going beyond just income. The new classification introduced in the 2010s looks at the education of the chief wage earner (CWE) and the number of durables owned. The latest classification looks at the occupation of the CWE and the qualifications of the most educated person in the home, irrespective of gender. These factors are needed because it has been found that segmenting only on the basis of income is often limiting.

When a consumer recognises a need, what do they do? Chances are that they will search their memory: 'I remember seeing this AC model in my friend's house, so we will go with that.' However, memory is not always enough and we end up asking friends and relatives: 'Hey, which 1.5-tonne split AC is the best?' And you would get a number of responses to go through. But in the digital age, all searches end up on the internet. Taking your list of recommendations, you will browse through options on e-commerce websites like Amazon or Flipkart. Savvy consumers may search for platforms where they can read reviews of products—automobile portals like Team-BHP have a vast treasure trove of consumer reviews to help a buyer decide, or a simple service like a pathology lab or a gym is often selected based on the reviews the consumer sees on Google Maps. Consumers today rely on reviews before making most buying decisions. And all smart brands and retailers track these reviews and respond to them in real time.

When asked, most consumers say that advertising plays no role in their final choice. But when asked about where they first heard of, say, Voltas AC, they may sheepishly admit that they saw an ad on

TV, but that, of course, is not influencing their choice. Marketers need to guard against such issues when trying to understand and decode consumer behaviour.

The growth of digital platforms is modifying consumer behaviour in many other ways. How consumers search for information or the way they buy a product has changed. In some categories like fashion and apparel, reports say that in 2023, more than 15 per cent of value sales occurred through e-commerce platforms. In the case of consumer products like soap and shampoos, the contribution of e-commerce platforms is growing fast and in 2023 was nearing 7–10 per cent, with some categories like diapers selling a much larger share through e-commerce platforms. Over the years, from 2020 to 2024, quick commerce (or q-commerce) has emerged as yet another way in which consumers buy products; some consumer-facing brands claim that q-commerce is generating even bigger sales than e-commerce for them.

With the growth of e-commerce and q-commerce, will all consumer buying migrate to digital platforms? In a vast country like India, that seems unlikely. There is the traditional general trade that has bounced back after the COVID-19 pandemic. Modern trade, which came up in the 2010s and was expected to overthrow general trade, has come nowhere close to doing this. It is likely all three—modern trade, general trade and e-commerce, including q-commerce—will continue but will vary in composition depending on the town class, product category and consumer typology.

Coming to consumer typology, a millennial or GenZ consumer may prefer buying anything and everything through e-commerce platforms. An older consumer may use digital platforms for information gathering but prefer to buy from a brick-and-mortar store. Here again, behaviour would differ with product type. Some young consumers may prefer to buy apparel through e-commerce, while some others would seek a physical shopping experience.

Regardless, the primary job of marketing is to understand who the target consumer is, how they go about buying the product or service and what value they derive from the purchase.

As we start understanding consumers and their buying process, we also need to figure out who is playing what role in the purchase and use of the product. In the mid-1970s, the purchase of any durable used in the home was done by the male head of the household. There is the famous Prestige pressure cooker ad that shows a husband buying it as a display of his love for his wife ('Jo Biwi Se Kare Pyaar'); the wife who is shown in the ad is but a mute spectator in the transaction. But in most middle- and high-income homes today, essential household purchases are carried out by the person running the kitchen—in most cases, a woman. Whirlpool tapped this insight by creating a series of 'Whirlpool Mom' commercials targeting mothers. Of course, various people play multiple roles in a home—there is the person who senses the need, the person who pays for the purchase, the person who uses the product and so on. Every one of them has a role to play. Take the case of toothpaste. The women of the house may decide which brand to buy, but the kids may have 'veto' power. Hence, most toothpastes are formulated to ensure that kids love the taste.

When it comes to B2B purchases, the process is more complex, with a number of actors playing a variety of roles. The process is also a lot longer and may consist of the following steps: problem recognition, general need description, developing product specification, supplier/source search, request for information, request for proposal, proposal evaluation, negotiation process, selection, formal transaction and evaluation of transaction. B2B marketing companies have to understand the various organisational buying centres (OBCs) and what role they play in the purchase and use of a product or service. The OBCs could include the user department, the engineering department, the purchase department, the finance department and so on. In the case of big capital equipment purchases, even the CEO may get involved. Good B2B companies try and map the benefits offered by their products' various OBCs. Each of these OBCs may have their own criteria for selection: the purchase department is interested in keeping the price low or the user department, for machinery, may be interested in smooth running of the machine with minimum downtime regardless of cost.

B2B marketing companies have realised that the more time is spent on understanding the organisational buying process, the better the chances of success in the final bidding war.

Over the last decade, the growth of digital information sources have changed the typical 'need recognition-search for options-evaluation of options-purchase-post purchase' funnel. Today, we speak of a customer decision journey (CDJ), where the customer may add or delete brands as they go through a search process. They may start with looking at three brands of cars before buying a small car. They may visit three or four showrooms. Then they spend time on the automobile portals and perhaps discover two new models. They may then add those two to the shortlist and go showroom-hopping again. They may ultimately end up buying a car model that was not even on their initial list. In such a case, a brand at the top of the funnel when the search started may not reach the bottom of the funnel. This poses a new challenge to marketers. Not only do we have to get the product into the consideration set (with which the customer starts out) but we have to ensure that we don't lose the prospect along the CDJ. Understanding the CDJ and engaging with the consumer through it is now critical for long-term brand success. No wonder car dealers grab our mobile numbers and email IDs when we take a test drive so that they can follow up with us throughout our journey!

The consumer decision journey is constantly changing, and is exciting to study. For example, if you are marketing a prescription product for hair fall and your target prescriber is a dermatologist, whose journey will you map? The doctor's? Or that of the patient, who may only come to the dermatologist after the case becomes too difficult to cure?

Given the many complexities involved, it might appear that understanding consumers is well-nigh impossible. But in order to succeed in marketing, you have to spend time and effort in figuring out the behaviour of the typical consumer and the buying process, even if it is not possible to cover all segments.

Having worked across a variety of products and services, I am keenly aware that consumer behaviour is dependent on the type of product you are selling and the reputation of the brand. Buying a pack of potato chips is not the same as buying a car or a smartphone. The way a teenager will go about buying a pair of jeans will be different from the way their mother will buy a sari.

> 'It is not just about asking a consumer ... it is about looking at the behaviour that gives you a lot of learning.'
>
> *—Pavan Sarda, Group CMO, Digital/Marketing/E-Comm, Future Group*

How Many Consumers Are There?

Before we start spending money in commissioning consumer research projects, we need to find out what information is available internally. Companies often have data lying with various other departments that is not shared with the marketing team. Analysing internal information can give us an idea about where our consumers are and where they can come from.

Then comes information that could be in the public domain, either freely accessible or available for a small fee. In several categories, there are reports about the size of the market or the composition of segments. Some of these, like the Euromonitor or the Centre for Monitoring Indian Economy (CMIE) reports, may cost you a significant amount, but that is still be a fraction of what you will spend if you were to do the digging yourself. Reports like the National Family Health Survey (NFHS) are issued at regular intervals and can be a treasure trove of consumer information, such as health practices and food habits. The Census of India is a source of information that can be tapped to map and understand various states and districts of India. Based on the NFHS and census, several other reports are available for you to understand the number of consumers and how they are distributed.

India also has a vibrant media ecosystem that throws up useful information about consumers and their media habits. Surveys like the Indian Readership Survey are also used to collect product- and brand-level user data. These help media owners sell in a more targeted fashion to potential advertisers. Television media companies also carry out their own versions of large-scale audience surveys that collect information about households. All these can be of use to a marketer.

The most commonly used secondary sources of information for consumer products is the retail sales data garnered through the retail audit. These can tell you about the size of the market, competitive market shares, distribution penetration, stocking levels, etc. If retail audits tell you about the sales of products through outlets, who is buying and using the products? Here is where consumer panel data comes in. Consumer panel data tells us who is buying the product, how often they buy it, what brand they used a month ago and so on. Both retail audit reports and consumer panel reports are available for a range of consumer products. Most other categories have their own version of retail sales audits. For example, automotive companies have their association, SIAM, that puts out monthly sales reports. Many of these reports require subscriptions to access. And the greater the granularity you need (statewise data, for example), the more it will cost you.

A detailed study of these secondary sources of information will help you develop some hypothesis about the consumer. What products do they use? What is their brand loyalty? How often do they buy?

For example, if we are looking at the potential for a hair fall product, secondary sources and retail panel data will give us an idea of the size of the overall market, the segments that are growing, the states that offer the most potential, etc. All this can be done without spending big bucks on a research study. If you want to understand what doctors do when a patient complains about hair fall, you will have to refer to the prescription audit for more information.

In this digital age, there is a treasure trove of consumer information that is available about all kinds of products. Consumers are encouraged to post reviews, which is information you can analyse. If you are setting up a medical diagnostics lab, you can search on Google and find the reviews of the labs near your location. Amazon and Flipkart also offer a vast amount of consumer reviews, both negative and positive. You may be able to pick up interesting patterns from the reviews. Of course, not every consumer will post a review and chances are that a disgruntled consumer may be more inclined to posting a negative review, but it's worth analysing nonetheless.

Digital platforms also offer a window to experts and what they feel about products. Many experts have blog posts that review products. For example, if you are interested in understanding hair care and what experts have to say about the current range of brands, you can do that by visiting various websites and platforms where experts and influencers post their views.

The growth of generative artificial intelligence (Gen AI) will offer further help to marketers. For example, if you have thousands of reviews of your brand on social media or e-commerce platforms, you can gather and upload them on to a Gen AI tool to be analysed. You could do the same with the consumer reviews of your competitors. What would have taken you several weeks of work might be done in a few hours or less.

With the boom in digital information sources, you can, sitting at your desk, develop some very useful hypothesis about consumers. Obviously not all of them may turn out to be true. A lot more work is still to be done on your journey of unearthing valuable consumer insights.

What Is in the Consumer's Mind?

You have carried out your internal immersion with consumers. You have looked at the market information through secondary sources like news reports, retail panel data, consumer panel data, digital immersion, review analysis, etc. All this may give you a good idea about the potential for your product. But you may want to know more about consumers, about how they research and buy. Your own home visits and shop visits may present a biased view. Now comes the important step of using an external market research agency to speak with consumers.

Before you start any kind of research that will cost you serious money, you should complete the secondary data analysis and your own dipstick. These two critical stages will hopefully answer some of your questions. But more importantly they will provide you with the information gap you need to fill with your paid research projects.

Any research project starts with articulating a few key questions:

- Who is the target consumer?
- What is the product or service you want to find out about?
- What are the information areas to explore?
- What kind of early hypotheses do you have?
- What kind of stimulus do you plan to use in the research exercise?

Qualitative research, as the name signifies, is more exploratory in nature. Qualitative research cannot prove or disprove your hypotheses. For example, if your hypothesis is that fuel efficiency is the most important criterion when buying a hatchback car, this cannot be proven or disproven through qualitative research. It can, however, provide you with a broad understanding about the consumer. While we do use a questionnaire in qualitative research, the questions are mostly open-ended, such as 'What do you do to control your weight?' versus close-ended multiple choice question such as:

> Of the following, which are the methods that you use for weight control?
> - Avoid sugar
> - Exercise
> - Cut down on simple carbs like rice
> - Cut down on oil
> - All the above

Given the set of questions you go with, qualitative research will open up new areas for you to explore in your quantitative research.

What Are the Broad Types of Qualitative Research?

The most common form of qualitative research is the focus group or focus group discussion (FGD). Here, a set of consumers are invited to a central location and a well-trained moderator conducts a discussion among them around the product category. In order to avoid bias, consumers are not known to each other. They often belong to the same social class or gender group to avoid any other kind of influence. While the moderator is conducting the discussion, observers listen and watch the conversation from another room through CCTV. They can, if required, pass on some additional questions to the moderator as the FGD is in progress.

Conducting focus groups takes a lot of experience. A trained moderator would refer to the discussion guide only now and then, since running a group for ninety minutes and keeping the momentum going is a challenge. You need to watch out for participants who talk too much and those who don't speak at all. A good moderator builds on the conversation and gets everyone to speak, making course corrections as the discussion progresses while keeping an eye on the clock, listening to the answers, monitoring arguments and raising further questions.

There is this anecdote involving a brand manager. She was casually listening to the chatter among the women who had attended an FGD conducted by a professional agency, and realised they were speaking about a session they had attended the previous week and the one they would be attending the following week. Alarm bells rang. She called the FGD moderator and the coordinator/recruiter to reiterate that first, she had wanted people in the group who didn't know each other and that, second, she did not want 'professional FGD attendees'. The session was cancelled and a fresh group was organised the following day that met the criteria.

With the availability of digital technology, many market research agencies organise digital mini-focus groups (MFGs). These MFGs often consist of four consumers, all attending from their homes. The moderator oversees the session while observers monitor the proceedings on Zoom or any other platform and suggest questions to the moderator through the chat mode.

Are these digital MFGs as good as a face-to-face focus groups? It depends. One big advantage is the saving in travel expenses and time for a trained moderator. But the downside is that the group is very small and there are limitations in the kind of stimuli that can be used. For example, while doing a focus group in a central location, consumers can be made to interact with the product (like a cream or a mobile phone), asked to do a product-sorting exercise, given pictures of film stars or animals to play a 'match the picture with the brand' game and more. Digital MFGs don't provide for these benefits, though they save us a lot of time and money. While physical focus groups can run for two hours, MFGs have to be much shorter than that. But it is likely that new technologies will

How to test or not test ads. Credit: Funny Business, *Shobha Prasad*

soon enable MFGs to use projective techniques to elicit deeper responses from consumers.

The other key type of qualitative research is the depth interview (DI). Here, a consumer in interviewed in a free-wheeling format (with a broad set of questions) by a trained investigator. These conversations can run for 100 to 120 minutes depending on the level of interest evoked by the product category and the investigator's ability. While doing a DI, you can introduce stimuli like products, pictures, etc.

In both FGDs and DIs, we often use what is known as the 'inverted funnel' approach. If we want to study the use of cooking oil, the discussion may start at a broad level of food, what kind of food the family likes, who makes the food and so on, and then drill down to the choice of cooking oil.

While focus groups and depth interviews are held with typical consumers, you can also use these techniques to speak with experts. For example, in the food category, you may want to speak with home chefs and not just homemakers. In some cases, you can form a group of experts and run a longer session called an extended creativity group (ECG). While doing automotive research, you may want the consumers or experts to experience the vehicle (these types of sessions are called 'auto workshops'). A ready to cook brand may have the group in a kitchen set-up for the research. While doing research with working executives, you may organise the focus group as an evening get-together at a five-star hotel.

Qualitative research can also be observation studies. A research investigator may want to observe how a consumer goes about their daily chores, uses ingredients, cleans the home or maintains their wardrobe. This may not involve a big list of questions, but a few questions after quiet observation.

Ethnographic studies are used by anthropologists to study how societies function and conduct day-to-day business. Ethnographers are known to live in communities for weeks or months together to eliminate any research bias. In consumer research that draws on ethnographic concepts, the researcher does not ask questions but plays the role of a fly on the wall, often for hours or days together. There are research agencies that offer mini-ethnographic studies to help decode consumer behaviour and attitudes in an objective manner.

Observation studies are also used extensively to understand shopper behaviour. Who is a shopper? A shopper is a consumer or buyer who is in the process of shopping. A shopper may not be the end consumer but can be influenced to change their decision on what to purchase by suitable intervention at a certain point. How does a shopper or consumer go about buying items in a supermarket? Or how does a shopper or consumer go about looking at durables in a showroom? In digital spaces, e-commerce platforms can observe and track every single move a shopper or consumer makes.

Doing qualitative research calls for innovation and improvisation. For example, how do you study the relationship between kids of four or five years of age and their colouring tools, such as crayons? An innovative researcher decided to organise a fun colouring party at her home and invited ten of the neighbourhood kids to it. Observing the way the kids interacted with crayons and the conversation around the colours gave the marketing team interesting consumer insights. Another researcher wished to study how parents and kids interacted with ice cream, and she spent a few days at an ice cream parlour observing and speaking with consumers. Or how do you get consumers to speak about fresh juices? How about carrying several bottles of freshly squeezed orange juice to offer along with your own brand to the focus group discussion planned? By getting consumers to sample various products, you can get a very animated discussion on the topic of juices.

Internationally, consumers are compensated via cash vouchers for the time they spend participating in a group. This trend has started gaining ground in India too. While planning on doing qualitative research, you need to budget for this as well.

Depending on the product category you are working with, qualitative research is going to give you some useful information. But if you can use your imagination to create an interesting way to engage consumers, you may end up getting much more than what a standard focus group will unveil.

Your qualitative research may have thrown open several options. But since qualitative research is done with a limited number of consumers, you cannot extrapolate the results to the population. For instance, your four groups may have indicated that it is fuel efficiency that matters when buying a small car. Will this be true with the larger population? To find out, you will have to do a larger consumer research, which is what we call a quantitative study.

> 'As brand managers, you need to meet your customers because that is where you get your insights from.'
>
> *—Viju Nair, Commercial Director, Abbott Healthcare*

How to Decode Consumers for Marketing Action

The journey of understanding consumers has so far depended on an analysis of secondary information, your own immersion and well-planned external qualitative research. These three may give you broad answers to the questions you started out with, that is, who is the consumer? How do they go about buying the product? What are the influences on them? How do they rate various competing products? How do they react to my product's concept?

You may have reasonably good answers, but can you be sure about the findings? After all, through qualitative research you may have talked to thirty consumers through four FGDs.

This is where quantitative research comes in. Quantitative research, as the name suggests, is about speaking with a larger number of consumers so that you can confirm the early hypothesis derived from FGDs. Quantitative research is expected to reflect reality, and the results should be projectable to the population. For instance, through FGD, you found that your product's concept of a millet-based chip was well-liked by a handful of consumers. But how many will try the product? That can be answered only by doing a quantitative study with a larger sample size of maybe 500–1,000 consumers. There are several statistical tools available for you to predict with a certain level of confidence that what is said by the sample can be extrapolated to the population. In general, a bigger, randomly selected sample can give you greater levels of confidence. Even so, you should watch out for the fact that consumers may not finally behave the way they said they would (after all, election polls have often gone wrong for this reason).

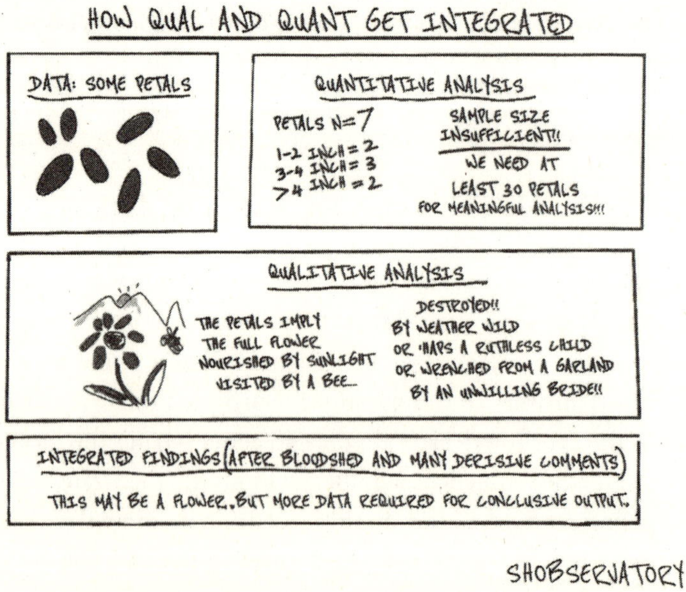

A humourous take on how qualitative and quantitative research get integrated. Credit: Funny Business, *Shobha Prasad*

While getting down to doing quantitative research, you need to start with the target consumer you want to interrogate. The next step is to define a sampling frame. For years, market research agencies in India have used electoral rolls to identify consumers and pick them on a random basis; if the city where the research is to be done is Nashik, the research agency uses its electoral rolls, randomly selects a few polling booths and then from those booths randomly chooses homes. Often they may follow a rule of picking every fifth home in an area. This elaborate method is used to ensure that the sample is totally random. Sometimes this may not be possible and you may want to adopt a convenient sampling method by meeting consumers in a bazaar or a shopping mall. In developed countries where telephone research was more common, the telephone directory was used to define the population, just as we used electoral rolls.

In India, we have traditionally used what is called face-to-face interviewing methodology, but that has changed in the last decade. Today, more research is done through telephonic interviews and through emails. But while a face-to-face interview can take twenty to thirty minutes, it is difficult to engage with a consumer on the phone for more than ten minutes, or if the email questionnaire is more than a few pages consumers may just drop off.

Good quantitative research has to be backed by a good research design. This will define the target respondent, the hypothesis, the information areas to be covered, the final analysis, etc.

The backbone of quantitative research is the questionnaire. A lot of time has to be spent on its design. Research agencies often pre-test the questionnaire several times before rolling it out. While planning the questionnaire, you need to be clear about how you will be analysing the data collected. Often, brand managers want multiple questions to be added, making the questionnaire unwieldy, then the data collected is not analysed in any meaningful way. Keeping the questionnaire concise is important; a compact questionnaire helps the investigator and the respondent.

Remember that there can be many a slip between the cup and the lip: data to information to insight is a difficult journey. As you are planning the questions, you need to ensure that the information you are collecting is both valid (true) and reliable (repeatable).

Quantitative research is prone to several types of errors. The first is the sampling error; this occurs when you select a sample that is not representative of the population. For example, carrying out research in a big city and then expecting the results to apply to small cities. Then there are non-sampling errors which occur due to mistakes in the questionnaire, misunderstanding of terms, etc. Just as in any type of qualitative research, we will have to factor in the respondent bias. Becoming a respondent in a survey could cause its own bias, that is, someone may want to answer the questions the way they think will make them look good.

Unlike FGDs, quantitative research is time-consuming and costly. You can run ten FGDs in four cities and get the results in four weeks or less. Quantitative research done with 1,000 consumer across ten cities will take a lot more time and effort. In many product categories, the investigators have to be trained to ask questions in the local language, field supervisors have to do random checks to ensure that the consumer has really been spoken to, etc.

Several research agencies nowadays are in a position to do telephonic and/or email interviews. These are, of course, a lot quicker and less expensive. But the information that can be garnered through face-to-face interviews is always a lot richer. Given the cost and time pressures, chances are that in the future in India too we will see fewer research projects using such interviews. Perhaps technology will make face-to-face interviews more efficient. Agencies are already using smartphones and tablets to simplify such interviews. Large consumer databases are available and questionnaires can be delivered to random sets of consumers via their smartphones or laptop in a few seconds, for which they are rewarded with gift vouchers. Results are available in a few days. There are, however, restrictions on the questions and the prompts you can use. But there are sure to be solutions for those too. Interestingly, the backend offices of several large global marketing research agencies are based in India. These offices prepare, deliver and analyse large global studies.

Types of Quantitative Research

There are multiple types of quantitative research that are used by organisations to understand consumers, one of which is known as the usage and attitudes study (U&A).

A U&A study looks at consumer's usage of a product class and their attitudes towards multiple brands. A typical U&A study for a consumer brand like a shampoo would start with the awareness levels of brands, current usage and ever usage of various brands. For instance, for Sunsilk you may get top-of-mind (TOM) awareness of 12 per cent, unaided awareness (UA) of 75 per cent, aided awareness (AA) of 95 per cent, current usage (CU) of 10 per cent and ever usage (EU) of 25 per cent. This information by itself is not of great use, but when used with the data of a few leading competitors, you will be able to identify if there is an awareness problem, a trial problem or a repeat usage issue.

Let me illustrate with some fictional data:

Brand	Top-of-mind awareness	Unaided awareness	Aided awareness	Current Usage	Ever usage
Sunsilk	12	75	95	10	25
Chik	13	65	85	7	15

From the above data, a marketing executive can figure out the relative brand issues between Chik and Sunsilk. Why does Chik have a lower current usage compared to its TOM? Is there a quality issue? Or is there a trial issue, since only 15 per cent have ever used Chik? And so on.

A U&A study doesn't just end with this data. The study then goes on to ask consumers how they rate various attributes with respect to the product. If we go by shampoo, we may ask them to rate the importance of qualities such as fragrance, foaming, hair softening, hair fall reduction, value for money, etc. Once we know the ratings of consumers, we then need to find out how our brand stands across all these attributes vis-à-vis the leading competitors. A well-planned U&A study will answer many questions about the health of our brand: where it stands with respect to the competition, what are its strengths and vulnerabilities, what are the competitive threats, etc. Many brands conduct large-scale U&A studies every two or three years. Often, these studies are preceded by several qualitative research studies.

But if U&A studies are done once every few years, how do companies monitor brand health on an ongoing basis? One way is via brand-tracking studies. While U&A is done with a large sample across multiple centres, brand-tracking studies are done in a few towns on a monthly or quarterly basis. Brand tracking should tell us about the consumer awareness of our brand and their image of our brand versus our competition. These studies are shorter and easier to administer.

Most B2C brands manage to keep track of their consumers by using a combination of retail panel data, consumer panel data, digital listening, qualitative research, brand-tracking studies and larger U&A studies. Better managed organisations maintain an impressive array of metrics that encompass both the physical and virtual world of brands. Some of the data is collected in real time. If you are a brand with a digital presence, you will be tracking the number of unique visitors to your website, time spent, where the visitors came from, what they looked at, etc. In this regard, an e-commerce platform like Amazon has a plethora of information about consumer behaviour, which they share with their vendors and brands. They also actively monetise the advertising potential of their website to the extent that e-commerce sites are emerging as the ZMOT or Zero Moment of Truth ad platforms, much like Google Ad Words.

If you think B2B brands don't do any of this, you are mistaken. Even in B2B situations, there is a need to understand consumers or customers and prospects better. Many companies conduct regular C-Sat or consumer satisfaction surveys, which help in understanding how your current customers are rating your performance. Bain & Co pioneered the concept of NPS or net promoter scores. Here, the customer is asked to answer just one question, 'On a scale of one to ten, how likely are you to recommend the brand to friends and family?' People who choose nine or ten are called your 'promoters', those choosing six or below are called the 'detractors', those giving you seven or eight are just 'passives'. NPS is calculated by subtracting the numbers of detractors from the numbers who are your promoters. So if 40 per cent are promoters, 40 per cent are passives and 20 per cent are detractors, your NPS is 20. Many companies have found the use of NPS very useful to monitor ongoing customer engagement.

B2B marketing companies also conduct large-scale usage and image studies. But as can be expected, the use of marketing research and consumer research is wider in B2C businesses. Most B2B companies believe that they are in direct contact with their customers and prospects, and that there is no need to do any third-party marketing research. But the information that your own team collects can be so misleading, for instance, your customers and prospects may not be telling your team the truth or your team may want to polish some of the data they gather. As such, even in B2B marketing situations, there is a need for large-scale customer surveys.

If you are to take a company trying to develop a new product, where to do you start?

The first step of involving consumers in new product development could be through ideation workshops with them. For instance, you may want to engage with what are known as 'fringe' consumers. If you are developing a new type of shoe, you may want to speak with marathon runners and trekking enthusiasts, knowing fully well that your average consumer is not a marathon runner.

The next step is concept testing, where you develop three or four product concepts that are written on a concept card and shown to consumers. Some companies are happy doing a few FGDs, other companies want larger validation and do concept test studies with a big sample size as a quantitative study. The winning concept is then converted into the product. In many product categories, you can follow up the concept test with an actual product test where you can get consumers to try out the product and give you feedback.

Once you have the product, you can shift your focus to the marketing material. Ad testing is one way in which you can hone your marketing communication inputs. Draft television or video ads are created as animatics and shown to consumers to get a reaction. Several market research agencies have packaged ad testing methods that you can use. These research agencies have been ad testing for years and have a lot of data on what is a good score. They can give you an indication of which ad will work better (remember it is always better to test two or more ads).

These are just a few types of consumer research I have been involved with. A good researcher can add a lot of value by creating new ways of unearthing useful insights. As always, GIGO rules apply to consumer research too. If your research design is faulty, if your methodology is poor, if your questionnaire is unwieldy, you will get nothing at the end of a long-drawn-out research exercise.

Changing Consumer Understanding Domains

Consumer research methodologies like DIs, FGDs, ethnographic studies, observation studies and U&A have all been with us for decades. In the last decade or so, several new methods have emerged and more will with changing technology. For instance, neuromarketing is an area of science that studies how your brain reacts to stimuli. Why do we like some ads and hate others? Even while watching an ad, which part of it stimulates us more? If we ask a consumer, we will, of course, get some answers to these questions. But these are answers that the respondent might want us to hear. What if we can study their brain when they are watching an ad or looking at packaging design? By using electroencephalography (EEG), we can pick up the cues directly from the brain, instead of asking the consumers. Researchers get consumers to wear a cap that has many electrodes to measure the brain activity; consumers then watch ads and TV shows. As they do so, their brainwaves are analysed to find out what they liked or disliked. By using neuromarketing, companies have been able to create new edits of ads or redesign packaging, although such techniques are expensive.

With the proliferation of e-commerce sites, customer review sites and platforms, there is a whole lot of information that can be scraped from the net and used. The availability of AI and large language models (LLMs) can further aid our ability to do consumer research. We may be able to get an AI tool to rapidly summarise and analyse product reviews and suggest ways of improvement. Will these be perfect? Not really. For example, while working on a luxury apartment project, I used ChatGPT to tell me the top hundred special features that luxury housing developers are offering in India. I then asked ChatGPT to suggest ten new ideas. Were they all great? No, but I did learn something new.

As technology develops, we should be able to conduct FGD in spaces like the Metaverse and interact with consumers as we do in real life. Car companies are already doing launches in virtual reality. What is stopping them from conducting car clinics with consumers, displaying new models, new features and so on?

Summing Up

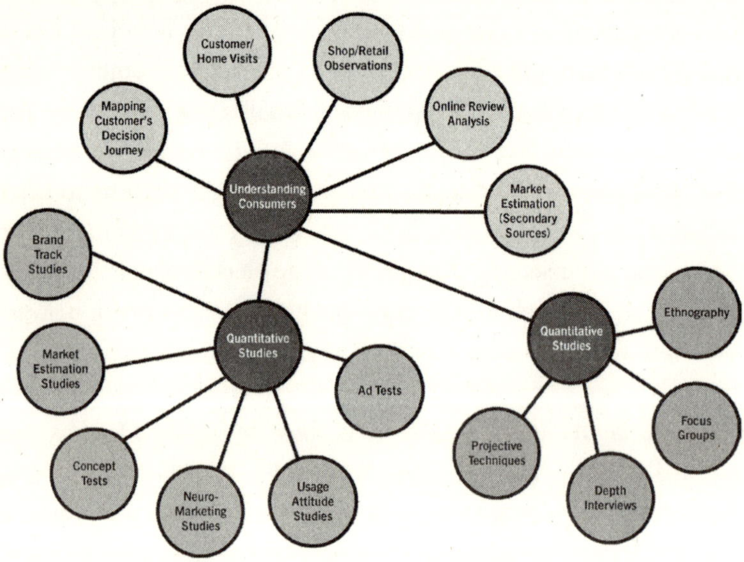

The many facets of understanding consumers

Successful marketing hinges on understanding consumers and unearthing powerful insights. A seasoned marketer knows that data has to be converted into information and information has to be analysed to become knowledge. From knowledge, we derive insights. For soap, the insight was 'Women want to look young'; for a nutritional supplement, the insight was 'Mothers are always worried that their child does not eat enough'; for a motorcycle brand, it was 'Fuel efficiency is needed most by a buyer of a commuter bike'. All these insights were acquired after a lot of information was churned and knowledge was extracted. Well-planned consumer research played an important role in the development of these insights which have built huge brands. Santoor. Pediasure. Hero Honda.

There is no one-size-fits-all approach when it comes to understanding consumers. What may work well in one category may not do so in another. What is true for one type of consumer may not be relevant for another consumer segment. Add to this how consumers are constantly changing in the ways they go about buying products and services.

The proliferation of smartphones has created new ways in which customers will consume content and shop. Digital brands are constantly monitoring consumer behaviour on their apps and websites. They can predict which consumer will buy what and when, almost telepathically. This is consumer understanding on another level. How many consumers come to our website or app? How long do they spend on our site? What are they looking at? What did they put in the shopping basket? What did they buy or not buy? From this data, what can we conclude? These are the questions that e-commerce brands are constantly studying. A little tweak in a sentence or a different picture can change the purchase metrics. Experimentation is the order of the day. Digital native brands are running hundreds of experiments all the time.

The data that is analysed is all about behaviour. What is causing the behaviour? What makes a consumer click or not click? The reasons may remain conjecture unless we are able to engage with consumers through qualitative and quantitative research. Consumer research is needed to decode the 'why'. And if you want to study where your brand stands in the market, you will need to engage with consumers of your brand and those of your competition. It may be possible that, by using a large data set and juxtaposing multiple hypothesis, you may be able to unearth some hidden reasons. If you add a dose of real consumer research, that is, speaking with consumers rather than relying on your own gut feel, you will definitely discover interesting consumer insights.

Understanding consumers is an essential marketing skill. In the age of digital marketing and big data, it can be very tempting to ignore the 'real consumer' and focus on just the data that is churned out. Intelligent marketing professionals do both—understand data and also understand the consumers.

But the most intelligent marketing professional will be able distil information from data and then use it to generate knowledgeable insights that will work for their brand. They will be the ones to shape consumer behaviour.

> 'If you don't change, the customer will change you.'
>
> *—Santosh Iyer, VP, Sales Marketing, Mercedes Benz India*

From the smallest of organisations to the biggest, good marketing mixology cannot happen without a deep knowledge of consumers.

2

The Magic Potion: Brand Building

A brand for a company is like a reputation for a person. You earn reputation by trying to do hard things well.

—*Jeff Bezos*

'Sir, I read your interview in *Dainik Jagran* and felt that you explained the concept of branding very well. I am calling from Bhopal, and we are manufacturers of masalas. We want to build a brand. Can you help?'

'One of our start-up friends recommended you. We are in the process of launching a very innovative educational toy. We want to understand how to build our brand and generate up to ₹100 crore in three years. Can you help?'

'We are a B2B company. We know our customers and our potential customers. But we are not good at marketing. Do you think we will benefit if our brand marketing is better?'

'Our brand team is doing a lot of work with data but I think they are not getting the big picture on branding. Can you work with them to help them untangle themselves from all the data and understand branding better?'

The first three questions were from businessmen and entrepreneurs who approached me to help them figure out the formula to the magic potion called 'brand building'. The last question was posed by the CEO of a large company who wanted me to help their talented brand team figure out what will work for which brand in their portfolio.

Interest in Branding

Why is there so much interest in branding? And why this desire to unlock the magic formula?

A visit to the local kirana may answer your question. Try selling a new product to the shop owner. The first question the shopkeeper would ask is, '*Kya brand bechthe ho?*' (Which brand are you selling?). Earlier, the second question used to be, '*Iska ad TV par aata hai kya?*' (Do its ads come on TV?). Nowadays they are more likely to ask, '*Consumer demand ke liye kya karte ho?*' (What are you doing to stimulate demand?)

From the smallest shopkeeper to the biggest business tycoon, all understand the power of the brand. The belief is that as against selling a generic product, a brand can help you earn profitable returns. You will be able to charge a higher price and make better profits. You will gain more acceptance from the retailer. Your customer (if B2B) will take your calls if your brand is known to them. A company marketing well-known brands will attract superior talent. A vendor will be keener to supply to a company that makes well-known brands. And finally, the investor community appreciates a company that houses well-regarded brands.

Twenty years ago, there was a debate as to whether consumers would continue to pay more for a brand that was almost identical to another. A book called *No Logo* became an instant bestseller.

The argument it posed was that as consumers learn more about the real cost of making products, they will gravitate to the best value offering. This was not a new theory. In the 1970s, when supermarkets in the UK and US were getting ready to offer their 'own label' products, there was a fear that premium-priced brands would fall by the wayside. 'Why would a consumer pay a 20 or 30 per cent premium for a Kellogg's cornflakes when Tesco cornflakes are available on the same shelf?' was the question. But this has not happened. Partly because of consumer inertia but also because brands help consumers save time and effort. Imagine every time you go shopping you have to experiment with new brands. You will spend hours reading packaging labels and have very little time to do anything else.

Brands Love Consumers and Vice Versa

Brands are here to stay. And that is the truth.

The first big myth about brand building is that it is very, very expensive to build a brand and that only big companies can do it. In reality, branding expenses can be tailored to suit your budget. Often the same resources used to make your product can be used to help you take baby steps to build your brand. Imagine you are the aforementioned masala manufacturer. If you want to build a brand, you can try and incorporate elements of what you want to communicate on your packaging. At zero extra cost. The poster you put up at shops can reflect the brand benefits instead of being some unconnected text matter.

The second myth is that brand building is very complicated. In a country like India, you can get overwhelmed by the large population, multiple states, multiple languages and multiple channels. But you don't have to launch the product pan-India. Several brands have been built by focusing their efforts in narrow geographies. What if the masala maker works only in Bhopal, and then in the state of Madhya Pradesh before venturing out?

The third myth is that of financial returns. This is further enhanced when we look at the cash burn rates of contemporary start-up companies. Some of them tote up losses that are higher than their sales revenue. Obviously, they know something that we don't know. There is also an abundant supply of cheap capital for them to burn and they have managed to sell a story to their venture capital investors: 'Our sales graph will spike the moment we cross a penetration of 10 per cent' or 'Sales will take off the moment our app's downloads exceed a crore.' Regardless, if you don't have an abundant supply of free cash, don't despair. Sensible branding can be done within any given budget. Successful brands have been built in this country using tried-and-tested rational brand investments and without the venture capital cash fountain.

The fourth myth is that branding is very long-term and only the Cokes, Pepsis, P&Gs and Unilevers of the world know how to do it, or that you need a person with an MBA degree from an IIM to do your branding for you. Not true at all. Some of the most successful Indian brands have been built by our own entrepreneurs. And in no particular order, here are a few brands that you may have interacted with: Balaji Wafers, Moov Balm, Ramraj Cotton, Lijjat Papad, Manyavar, V John, Paragon Chappals, Ajanta Clocks, D'Decor, Chik Shampoo, MTR Masalas, FabIndia, HiDesign, Kama Ayurveda, Zoho, Electral, Zodiac, Nirma … I can go on and on. All these brands have had humble beginnings and have managed to grab national attention after arduous brand building efforts.

> 'A good marketer needs to be a brand historian ... know the tipping points up or down and really understand what made them happen.'
>
> —*Sumit Mathur, Director, Marketing, Kellogg's, South Asia*

Mastering Branding Is for Everyone

I hope you are now convinced that brand building is not beyond the reach of a small- or a mid-sized entrepreneur.

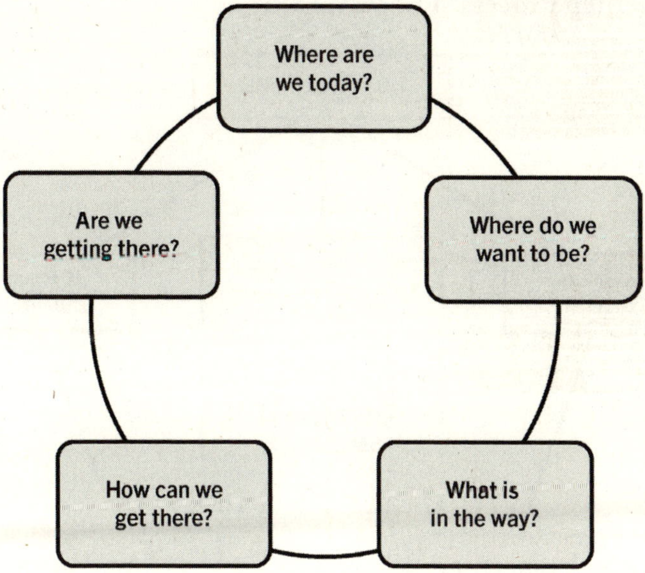

The brand planning process

Even if you do think you know branding, you may benefit from a quick crash course on branding basics.

This chapter has been tailored to help you navigate the branding journey irrespective of your starting point. You may be just about ready to create a new brand. Or you may have inherited a brand from your family. Or you may be in a business school, dreading the 500-page textbook on branding. Or you are working with a large company with several brand managers, but you want to ensure that you brush up on your skills and tools at regular intervals. Building a brand starts with asking several questions: Where are we today? Where do we want to be? What is in the way? How can we get there? Are we getting there? Often called the brand-planning cycle, it is the starting point of the creation of the brand magic potion.

Now get ready to brew the magic potion.

Five-Step Process: The Pentagon

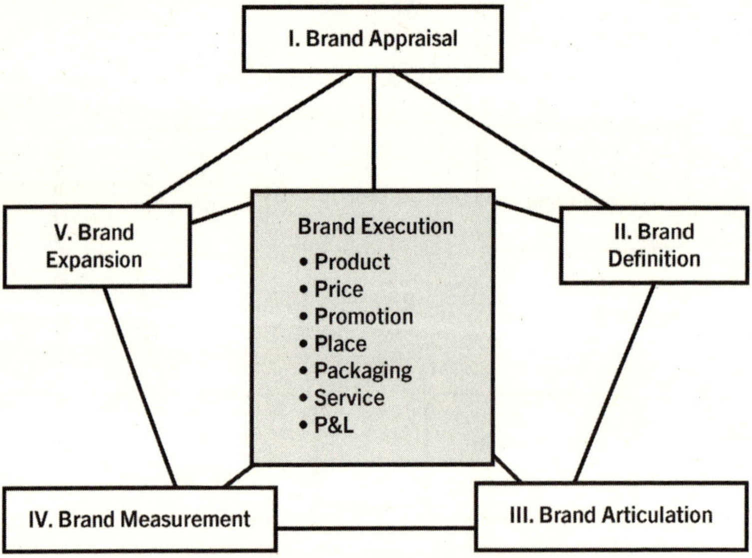

A pentagon on how to build your brand

The first step is what we will call **brand appraisal**. In this stage, we figure out if there is potential for a new brand (and the real potential of the brand we have at hand). We also establish who will be our consumers as well as our competition. Finally, do we have the competencies to take on the task? Brand appraisal consists of the analyses of the market, the competition, the consumer, competency and the socio-economic environment.

We have gathered the ingredients for the potion.

The next step is to figure out how the new brand will be pitched, that is, **brand definition**. How would we define our brand? Who would the brand be aimed at? What would the brand positioning be? This stage is critical since a brand cannot be many things to many people. The greater the focus you bring to your branding task, the greater the chance of success. At this stage, we must also decide on the broad contours of the Ps of marketing (product, price, promotion, place, process, people and packaging) as well.

The vat is ready and you have the ingredients in the right proportion. It's ready to brew.

The third step is to decide how you want the brand to be presented, that is, **brand articulation**. What would the brand name be? What will the brand logo be like, which colours will be used? We spoke about achieving branding at no cost. This is achieved by using your current packaging—to tell your brand's story better. Following choice of brand name and logo identity, we need to develop a brand communication plan. This could be advertising or public relations or sampling promotion or literature or website or digital advertising. In this stage, one has to take a call on how much to invest in the brand's marketing.

The first three steps are ideal for you if you are starting out on your branding journey.

What if you already have a brand? A brand that was introduced by your grandfather? Or a brand that has been in existence gathering dust in a long-forgotten corner of your company?

Irrespective of the origin or age of your brand, if you want to do what we call **zero-base brand planning**, you need to start with brand appraisal. Zero-base brand planning assumes that you are starting from scratch. You have inherited nothing except may be the name and the product formulation. When you do zero-base brand planning, there are no holy cows—you are going to get into critical thinking hyperdrive. You are going to question all assumptions. Why is the pack blue? Why are we saying 'all natural' on the pack? Why are we selling only to the pharmacy channels? Why are we selling to retailers when online is so much more profitable?

You are required to do brand appraisal, definition and articulation irrespective of where you are starting the journey. These steps are needed regardless of whether your brand is new or old, successful or struggling.

The brand has been created or recreated. Your herbs are all in the pot. The potion is boiling. The next crucial step is to test it, that is, **brand measurement**. Sometimes, companies complain that there is no need for this since they know the results from the sales' receipts. That may not be always true. For instance, if you are a long-gestation B2B marketer, your sales may take months to fructify. How do you know if your brand strategy is working? Or your sales have not increased, yet your brand strategy could be working. What if the market has collapsed but your sales are steady? Or what if there is a big new entrant, and your competitors have packed up while your sales are ticking? When you set up a robust brand measurement system, you also need to understand other metrics that you may want to measure. For instance, awareness levels with consumers and retailers, or image scores with potential users.

The potion has been tested. Your brand is doing well. What next?

The fifth step is what I call **brand expansion**. You have made your brand a success. What do you want to do with your brand? Will you expand it into new geographies? Or will you introduce new products under the same brand?

This is the five-step process for brewing the brand magic potion.

Let us now start the journey by diving deeper into each of the stages.

1. Brand Appraisal: Picking the Ingredients

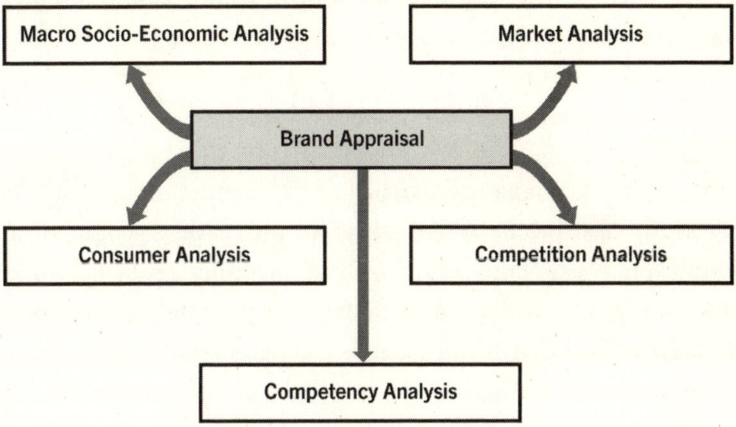

The components of brand appraisal

How do you start making the magic potion? Do you just start by boiling random herbs or do you find out what the potion has to do and for whom? What can they afford to pay you for the potion? In the case of the comic book *Asterix the Gaul*, the magic potion has to give super-strength to the villagers to save their homes from the marauding invaders.

You, too, need to understand what the purpose of the branding exercise is and what you want to achieve. If you already have a brand, or what you think is a brand, you need to hit the pause button and go back a few steps to do a brand appraisal.

If you are a start-up thinking of a ready-to-eat (RTE) food product, do you just have a bright idea one day and launch it the next day? Or do you want to do some preparation before you launch it?

The first stage consists of a few sub-parts such as the analyses of the market, the competition, the consumer, competency and the socio-economic environment.

If this looks like too much work, then you can stop right here and go back to what you were doing with your brand. But if you want to prepare the ground for bigger success, read on.

i. Market Analysis: Is there a market?

First, we try and identify the size of the market, how widely it is spread, what has been the growth of the market, geographical spread, price segments, etc. If you are planning on launching a new masala, you may begin by finding out the total consumption of masalas. But that is not enough. You may want to go further by understanding the sizes of branded and unbranded masala powders markets. What are the particular types that are sold and in which markets? Are there clear price segments, and how are they performing? Is there any seasonality with masala consumption?

Where do you get all this data? Some of the data for your category may be available in the open domain. You might have to otherwise invest in buying syndicated market information. Better to spend the money now than discover that the market estimates were wrong after launching your brand.

This first stage of analysis will tell you something about the size of the market and if there are gaps in the market. But also remember: there may be gaps in it, but there may not be any market in the gaps. For instance, there is possibly a market for a small motorised two-wheeler between a cycle and a motorbike. Some years ago, a south Indian two-wheeler manufacturer launched a 30cc bike. But it failed to take off. There was no market in the gap they had identified. In all likelihood, they had underestimated the power of the second-hand two-wheeler market. Will you buy a 30cc bike that can carry only one person or spend a little more and get a second-hand 100cc bike? (Interestingly, the boom in delivery services has created a market for small electric bikes and rent-a-bike brands).

ii. Competition Analysis: Where's the competition?

When you carry out market analysis, you will discover that there are a few key competitors whom you need to learn about. If you are operating in one state, you may have some national players and several local players. Each may have their own strengths and weaknesses. Who are the key competitors and what makes them successful? This is a very important area to get into. A lot of competitive information should be available online but don't underestimate the knowledge you can gain from spending time talking with retailers and distributors. You will know about the competition from their point of view.

iii. Competency Analysis: Do we know how to make it?

You have analysed the competition and the market; time for you to see where you stand. We call this competency analysis. What are your strengths? What makes you think you can succeed? When Tata Motors (or TELCO, as it was known) had wanted to enter the automobile market with Tata Indica, they knew that they had to win with a diesel model simply because they knew how to make diesel engines. That was their competency. So, what is your competency? It could be that you have deep knowledge of your local market and local taste. You may know how to make a masala just how consumers want it. You may be a tech-savvy start-up that knows how to create a technical solution for a complex enterprise resource planning (ERP) problem. That is your competency. So, understand and articulate your competency—and be aware of your limitations.

iv. Consumer Analysis: Will people buy our product?

The next step is consumer analysis. Who is the consumer and how do they go about buying the product category? Are there influencers who are critical for you to win over? If, for instance, you are launching a new battery for motorcycles, you need to not only understand the average bike buyer but also the motorbike mechanic's psyche. Or a paint company would have to understand the painter's mentality. Consumer analysis will also involve a deeper dive into two critical areas: penetration and consumption.

If, for example, you are planning to launch an RTE food brand, then you may want to find out what percentage of consumers today buy any RTE food product, from Maggi to MTR and ID. The numbers will vary from city to city and by socio-economic class. You may find that in urban upper-income households, the penetration, that is, at least one product's usage, is as high as 75 per cent. But in smaller cities, penetration may be only 25 per cent. Once you have a fix on penetration, the next question to ask is the frequency of usage. In India, penetration of many products is high but per-capita usage is very low. So a consumer who says they use RTE brand could be using it just once a month or once a week. In the US, for instance, research has shown that Kraft's Mac & Cheese is a staple food that is consumed by a large number of homes almost once a week or more.

Consumer analysis will help you map your consumer in terms of their demographics, income class, etc. You will have to match these segments with the two critical dimensions we spoke about: penetration and regularity of consumption. When Karsanbhai Patel launched Nirma, he knew that detergent powder was seen as very expensive by even middle-class housewives. At most, they used a detergent powder once a week, and opted to use a washing bar for their regular washing requirements.

In many categories, you may also encounter the problem of multiple uses of the same product. For instance, in lower-income homes, they may be using a washing powder like Nirma to mop the floor as well. They may be reusing the masala mix that comes with Maggi with their other foods. Indian housewives are indeed very innovative, so you need to not only understand what they are using but also where are they using it.

Consumer analysis is probably the most important step in your brand building journey.

v. Macro Socio-Economic Analysis: What's the weather like?

The country around us is changing and an analysis of macro socio-economic factors may throw up interesting trends. For instance, girls are keen on having a good education and pursuing a career. Hence, dual income households are on the rise. This in turn means that there will be an explosion in the need for baby day care services. A company spotted this opportunity and set up crèches in housing societies and IT parks. What a wonderful idea! Think again, what other opportunities will open up because of increasing incomes and working couples? There will be an explosion in the demand for gadgets that save time and effort. A chapati maker could be a much-needed appliance. Dishwashers could be the next big product to get a boost. In terms of consumer products, there is bound to be a big demand for food items that reduce the time and effort spent in daily cooking.

We only looked at working couples, but we know that all segments of Indian society are changing. There is a growing number of affluent elders and they have the money to enjoy their sunset years. Tour operators can create special tours for those wanting to tick things off their bucket list. Then there's also the fact that rural India is changing. Because of better connectivity via roads, satellite television and now mobile internet, there is bound to be a rapid growth of demand for a variety of products. How are you trying to tap this demand?

While I have presented the steps of brand appraisal in a sequence, let me assure you that this is not a rigid framework. You may work back and forth between some of the steps. For instance, we have the formula for an all-natural facewash that we want to relaunch after doing a full-scale analysis. We may start with a market analysis of the facewash market, then get to consumer analysis (the fourth step) but as we research, we find that consumers have different needs from their facewash brands. For instance, men may prefer a deep-cleaning facewash for use after a bike ride from office, while working women may like a gentler product. This may drive you back to market analysis. You may find that men use facewash but women prefer to use a gentle soap. Is there a bigger opportunity with men or women? Or should you look at a gender-neutral brand proposition? Be flexible with your approach.

2. Brand Definition: Preparing the Potion

> 'When you think about the distinctiveness of a brand and how it derives reference, Oreo is a very good case study.'
>
> —*Anil Viswanathan, Senior Director, Marketing, Mondelez India*

Before we work on defining a brand, we need to ensure that there is a gap in the market for it. Once this gap is established, we can move on to brand definition and look at how to craft a brand proposition to address the opportunity.

i. Brand Reasons: What's the raison d'etre?

The first stage in developing a brand definition is to establish the reason for its existence. Brand reasons could be rational, emotional and, nowadays, even social. A rational reason for a brand's existence could come from the ingredient it uses. For example, Vicco Vajradanti was promoted as an ayurvedic toothpaste. Fairever was promoted as a fairness cream with saffron. Or a brand could use an emotional reason to appeal to the consumer. Krack foot cream appealed to the pride of a woman to look good, head to toe. A social reason is where a brand appeals to a higher purpose. The brand Amul stands for the co-operative dairy farmer and ensures that you never forget the fact that it is not just another profit-making enterprise.

ii. Brand Positioning: Which mental slot to occupy?

The next critical stage in brand definition is the development of brand positioning. The analysis till now would have revealed the gap in the market, the unfulfilled needs of the consumer, the company's own competency, the competitive weakness and the changing socio-economic dynamics. How will you capture the brand promise in a simple statement? This is the all-powerful brand positioning statement (BPS).

The BPS has three critical elements. The first is the target consumer—who is the brand aimed at, what is their relationship with the product category, what are their current behaviours and what insights do we have about them? The second element is the single-minded promise that your brand offers—it must be said in a ten-word statement. Finally, the third element is the reason to believe—why should the consumer trust your claim?

A classical positioning statement will read as follows:

- For the consumer ______ (who may be male or female, who may be worried or dissatisfied about something),
- Brand XYZ is a ______ (the product category)
- Which ______ (the single-minded proposition)
- Because ______ (the reason to believe)

You should be able to write a simple positioning statement for a brand after watching a few good ads.

Let us try a few:

- For a young mother who is concerned about the growth of her baby
- Pampers diapers
- Will help her baby sleep and grow better
- Because babies who sleep better grow better, and Pampers keeps the baby dry for eight hours, ensuring continuous sleep.

or

- For a young man with a beard who wants to look dapper, stylish and well-groomed
- Beardo's range of beard accessories
- Will help manage the beard stylishly
- Because only Beardo uses natural emollients in its formulation and is available in a range of variants.

I am often asked a question—does a positioning statement matter to a small business? Of course it does. Every business operates with a positioning statement. The smarter companies know how to put it down as a guardrail to help them plan their strategy.

So irrespective of your business—it could be a product or a service, it could be national or regional or hyper local, it could be online or offline—you need to put down the positioning statement. It also has to be reflected in all that you do. And it should stay constant for a reasonably long period.

There are many positioning typologies. Let me list a few. Positioning can be based on ingredients (Dabur Amla hair oil), benefit (Zandu Balm), occasion of usage (Cadbury Dairy

Milk), feature (Fevistick), user (Marlboro), price (Nirma), value (Hyundai), tradition (Dabur), competition (B Natural), technology (Intel), simplicity of design (IKEA), country (L'Oréal), etc. Of course, while I have slotted a brand into a positioning typology cubicle, it offers more than just that. For instance, L'Oréal rides on its French origin but it also offers beauty because 'You are worth it'; Hyundai offers great value cars since their cars are well-designed and are comfortable to drive. So, just because you are over-compensating in one aspect, you cannot be weak in another.

iii. POP and POD: What's so different about us?

This leads us to the concept of point of parity (POP) and point of difference (POD). As you write your positioning statement, you have to be aware about the POP of your category. For instance, if you are a jeweller, you need to have a range of jewellery, a good showroom and well-trained staff. But your POD could be auspicious wedding jewellery. The jeweller GRT in Chennai is seen as a 'lucky' jeweller to buy wedding jewellery, for instance.

You are probably wondering when the 4 Ps of marketing will enter the argument. The BPS will determine the 4Ps—product, price, promotion and place. If you are targeting an upmarket consumer, you may go in for premium pricing and fancy packaging, or for exclusive online marketing. But if you want to go after the middle class, you may want to look at value pricing, wide distribution and so on.

iv. Brand Mapping: Do we have the full picture?

Once the BPS has been finalised, you may want to see how the brand will be visualised. What will the brand personality or image be like? Let us call this brand mapping. We have defined the brand with a very powerful BPS that can be undone if we don't define the brand map. What is the essence of the brand, what is the core and what is the extended personality of the brand—these are the next questions. Large companies use complex systems to define their brand, such as brand keys, a brand prism or a brand pyramid.

As you are ready to complete the brand definition exercise, it is important for you to take a step back and see if it makes sense. One good way of checking this is by doing some dipstick research. Of course, if you have the resources, you should do a proper detailed market research. This stage of market research is called 'concept testing'. You write out the BPS as a concept statement and show it to consumers to seek their reaction. In order to be able to eliminate research bias, always, always, test at least two concepts, and not more than that.

Brand concept testing can be tiresome for consumers.
Credit: Funny Business, *Shobha Prasad*

For instance, if you are planning to launch a new RTE upma mix but made with, say, an ingredient like sorghum (I have no idea if this is possible, so don't try it), we will have to create two types of BPS and concepts. Let us try two here:

1. For the young working professionals who want to start the day well, XYZ brand RTE upma will give you continuous energy for six whole hours because it contains the goodness of sorghum, which allows for controlled release of energy.
2. For the young working woman who want to start the day well, XYZ RTE upma will give you a great tasting boost in the morning since it contains sorghum, an excellent source of vital nutrients.

As is clear, brand building has multiple stages and you need to define the reasons for the existence of your brand, all derived from the appraisal that you have carried out. You then need to clearly articulate a BPS. Then you need to know what the brand map will be. Finally, before you head to the next stage, you need to stop and test if you are on the right page with your customers.

Even if you don't have enough resources to do an elaborate test, remember, you can use online forums to test concepts, like using Google Forms to run a test.

Once the results come back, you can then take a judgement call—you can either pick the option that scored higher and go with it, or the one that lost out but only by a small margin if you have a gut feeling that this is a winning concept. Back your gut feeling, unless it is seriously contradicted by research data.

Brand appraisal showed us the market gaps and needs. Brand positioning and testing concepts told us which recipe will produce the best results. Now we need to start boiling the pot.

> 'As the brand scales, you need to start thinking about driving relevance whereas earlier it was about imagery and aspiration.'
>
> —*Deepika Warrier, CMO, Diageo India*

3. Brand Articulation: Prepping the Potion

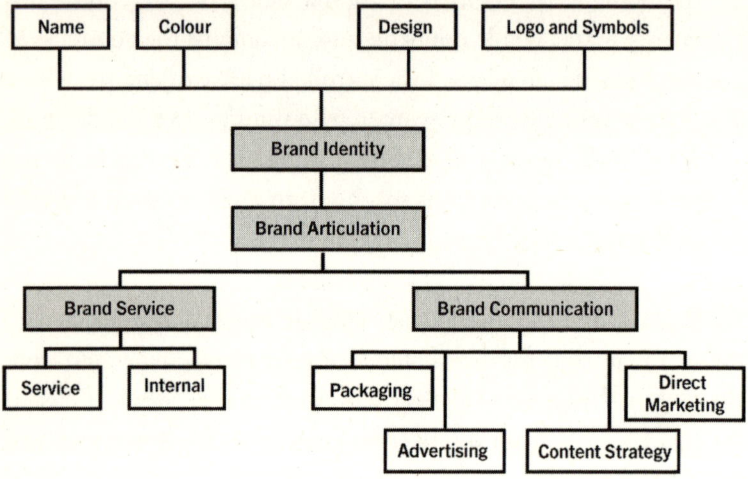

Brand articulation

However great your magic potion is, if you don't present it the right way, it may not have the desired effect. Imagine if the prasad at your local temple was served to you on a dirty plate? Presentation has its own effect and we need to be aware of it in all that we do.

Coming to the brand magic potion, we identified the recipe and the ingredients in the brand appraisal stage. Then we mixed them in the right proportion and created the brew in the brand definition stage. Now we come to the presentation of the potion. We will call this stage brand articulation.

Often entrepreneurs think of a brand name before deciding on the positioning. In some cases, the brand name may be inherited from the family. But if you have a choice, you need to hold the call on choosing a brand name till you finalise the BPS.

i. Brand Identity: How will our brand be presented?

Brand articulation starts with what we will call brand identity. The first thing about the identity is the name. What is a good name? The Bard of Avon (William Shakespeare, to the uninitiated) may have said that a rose by any other name would smell as sweet. But in reality, a good name can help give your business a boost. Is there a method to creating names?

First, the name should ideally flow from your brand strategy and your BPS. There are many typologies when it comes to creating brand names. Let us look at a few.

The first type of brand name is what we can call 'descriptive'. These names suggest what the product will deliver when used. CloseUp toothpaste will give you fresh breath. Itchguard will remove itches. Digene will help your digestion by reducing acidity. Burnol will soothe burns.

The second type of brand name is what we can call 'suggestive'. For instance, Apple creates computers that you can use as easily as you can say 'a for apple'. Visa is a credit card that lets you travel the world. Indica is India's car.

The third type of brand name is what we could call 'free standing'. These names may have nothing to do with the BPS. They could be family names like Birla or Tata. Or they could be a religious deity like Balaji or Ganesh. They could be unfamiliar words like Xerox, Kodak or Zee, or common words that get used for a totally different purpose such as Parachute coconut oil, Tortoise mosquito coil and Titan watches.

Interestingly, because of global language diversity, a brand name that may be descriptive in one country may become 'free standing' in another. 'Hamam' in Urdu or Turkish is the word for a bath; but chances are that the millions of Hamam soap users in Tamil Nadu have no idea about this. It seems Dabur Amla hair oil is a big seller in Egypt, but people there don't know what 'amla' means.

There are many stories about how a brand name in one language may end up sounding disastrous in another language. The Chevrolet Nova model ended up meaning 'it won't go' in Spanish (although the car did sell well in Latin America). As you decide on your brand name, you need to be aware of the problems you may face in a different part of the country. Brand names get truncated in India. Fair & Lovely was often referred to as 'Lovely' (in its new avatar of Glow & Lovely, it will probably get called 'Lovely' again). The candy brand Alpenliebe, a mouthful really, is referred to by retailers and kids as 'Liebe'.

Developing a brand identity also means deciding on the brand logo and what colours it will be presented in. Often small manufacturers miss out on this trick. They tend to use random colours across various packaging and lose out on the synergy they can derive if they stick to a colour template. Plus, this does not cost anything extra. Brand logo development is yet another important step and for a country like India, you need to visualise the logo in at least a few major Indian languages. Big brands do this very well. Check out how McDonald's or Dabur write their brand name in different Indian languages. Again, this is something that is inexpensive to execute and most small brands do not pay enough attention to this.

There was a time in India when all brands needed not just a brand name and a logo but also a symbol. This was critical since a large majority of consumers were illiterate (remember our political parties still use symbols in their sloganeering and often fight over the symbols when parties split). Rural and farm inputs were always promoted with a symbol. FACT fertiliser had elephants. Zuari had a man on a horse. Dalda had palm trees. Some of our brands were visually rich: Cheetah Fight match boxes; Wagh Bakri tea (tiger and goat tea; tea is a great leveller).

ii. *Brand Communication: How will our brand speak to consumers?*

Brand articulation starts with developing a brand identity, but once we have that, we need to take it to the market through communication. Developing a brand communication plan consists of four stages:

- Analysis
- Brief
- Creative idea
- Execution

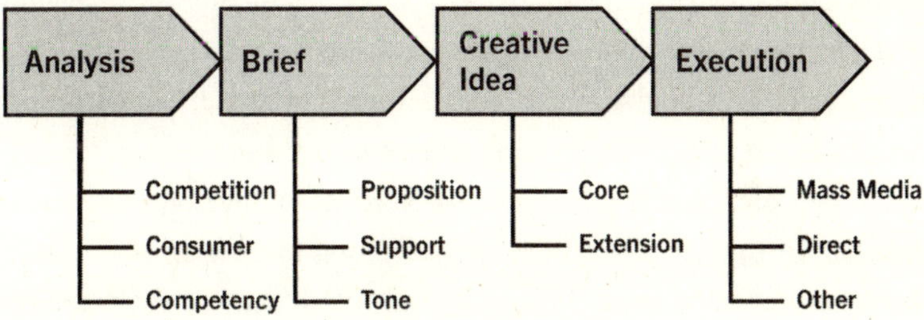

The roadmap to IMC development

Before we brief an ad agency, we need to put down the BPS and also give them a clear indication of the competition and the consumer—we call this analysis. Then we need to write a simple one-page brief that will consist of the target consumer, proposition, the support and the tone/manner (an expanded version of the BPS). The agency then develops the creative idea and the execution idea. Big companies have many agencies working with them on a single brand—creative, digital, media, activation and PR agencies (maybe more). A good way of possibly handling this circus is to make one of the agencies the 'lead agency' and tasking it with the job of finding the 'Big Idea'. The other agencies are then asked to follow that lead. For instance, if the product is a fabric softener, the creative agency may come with the idea of a fluffy cat. The other agencies are then told to take up the idea and execute it in their own domains.

Brand communication should start with the most basic of communications that a brand can do—its packaging. Sometimes packaging is developed and finalised well before the brand communication plans are in place, simply because it has a longer lead time. Ideally, well-integrated brand communication has the packaging at its centre.

In B2B marketing, brand articulation is given the short shrift. The general belief is that one-on-one selling is all that is needed. In today's digital world, it is hypercritical for a B2B brand to develop a BPS and ensure that all elements of communication align with that. This will include the brand name, website, presentation template, even the visiting card or e-card.

The digital age has enabled advertising to develop many new avatars. In the 1990s, most advertising was hinged on the thirty-second television spot. This was supported with print, outdoor, cinema and radio. Today, a successful brand communication plan may not hinge on television at all. You have multiple varieties of digital campaigns that you can use, from YouTube videos and Facebook, Twitter and Instagram posts to search marketing or influencer marketing.

If you are a big brand with a large budget, you can use all of these options as well as traditional media options like television and print. But even if you are a big brand, it makes sense to figure out how you want to commit your funds. Several big marketers have the 70:20:10 rule. They spend 70 per cent on tried-and-tested media. Then they spend 20 per cent on what is seen as somewhat unproven media. The final 10 per cent is for totally risky ventures. The Coke Studio partnership with MTV in India probably came out (in my view) from the 10 per cent budget kept for out-of-the-box ideas.

What if you are a small brand? How do you maximise your advertising budget? Here is where it makes sense to remember the 'paid–owned–earned' modalities of media. Paid media is what you pay for, so print, television and the YouTube videos you promote are all paid media. Owned media is what you own and is free for you—your own packaging, your vans, your shop exterior or, if you are a retailer, the walls inside your store. We don't fully realise the value of using owned media well. Finally, there is earned media, that is, the organic shares you may get if someone likes your ad or message. This is the most difficult of them all and is highly unpredictable. There is no guarantee that a video you produced so painstakingly will go viral. How can you improve your chance of success? Experts tell us that you need to keep running experiments all the time to improve your odds. Let us say you created a video with your product. Can you create two different versions of it, maybe three? Then you can run experiments and see which of these have a better chance of being shared organically. Sometimes a different typeface used in a social media post may deliver twice the returns. A change in the colour of the headline may improve response.

Before you run a campaign, it makes sense to test the ads. Here again, as we saw earlier, there is merit in testing two options. Big brands have figured out test methods that use what is called an 'animatic ad' (basically a video made with illustrations). You can even test simple boards which are just collages of various visuals. For instance, in the fabric softener example, we could test the cat visual against a dog visual and see which evokes a better response.

The entire market research industry is getting digitised and what was once a very laborious process can take place at a much faster rate. Purists do worry about the inability to randomise the responses, but the field of market research is changing rapidly and we should hopefully see that solved soon.

iii. The Three-Filter Stage: How do we pick the right message?

Brand articulation started with developing a brand identity and then went on to brand communication. The process today might be different from how it was decades ago, but some of the cardinal rules of advertising creative judgement remain. What you create, whether it is a television spot or a Facebook post, needs to be in alignment with the brand strategy and BPS—it has to be easy to understand, simple to communicate and, finally, campaign-worthy. We call these the three filters of creative judgement: brand filter, communication filter and campaign filter. Any creative you make will have to pass through these.

The problem that brands (especially big brands) encounter is that social media demands the creation of multiple messages every day. How does one ensure so many messages pass through the three filters? Amul has a wonderful series of hoardings that have been running for decades. It used to be only outdoor signages, but in the last ten years, these have been converted into engaging little ads in newspapers called Amul Topicals which also go up on all their social media handles. Almost every day, they create a message. Some of them go viral. Some of them remain ads. And very rarely they do get criticised. But, every day, they have to ensure the brand communication they create passes the triple filter test. Kudos to the brand and agency team for a job well done.

All service brands have yet another big challenge. They change every time a customer interacts with the brand. You order a coffee and the barista is rude—does that affect the brand of the coffee shop? You enter the department store and the store manager welcomes you by your name—how does that affect you? The challenge for a service brand is to ensure that every employee 'lives the brand'. They need to internalise the BPS of the brand and live it every day, during every interaction with a customer. Remember, every interaction is a 'moment of truth', and a brand can be made or broken at every interaction.

B2B brands use a different range of communication tools that may include conferences, exhibitions, etc. There is then the whole array of content that a B2B brand may employ, including websites, white papers, videos, etc. All these have to reflect the core of the B2B brand and cannot be stretched in different directions. If you have a B2B brand, then do study the masters like TCS, Infosys, BASF, GE, etc. An hour spent on their website will be worth its weight in gold.

(If all this was a little too confusing, relax. We will do a refresher of this in the chapter on communications.)

We have brought the brand magic potion to a boil. We added the right ingredients and we have cooked them to perfection. We have created anticipation about the effect of the potion. And we have delivered it with a golden ladle into silver bowls for consumption.

We now get to the stage of putting in some measurement metrics to see how well the potion is working.

> 'Balance between the functional aspect and the emotional aspect of the brand has to be managed.'
>
> —*Vivek Sharma, CMO, Pidilite Industries*

4. Brand Measurement: Evaluating the Potion's Effect

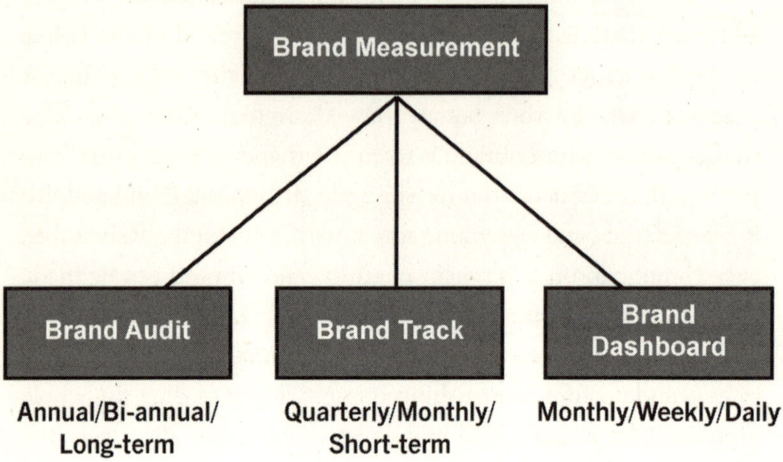

Measuring your brand

When you are launching your brand, you need to ensure that you put in place measurement metrics to see what is working and what is not.

A small businessman might say, 'What do I need to study? I know that my marketing and branding is working if my product sales improves. So the only metric that I need to measure is sales!'

A brand manager in a large company may say, 'Don't measure my branding efforts by the sales of my brand, but by the profits it is delivering. Ultimately, I am the managing director of my brand and my commitment is to deliver a healthy bottom line in the long run.'

Yet another businessman may say, 'I will know if my brand strategy is working if someone at a social gathering comes up to me and says he liked my latest ad.'

And, of course, there are those who measure success by the comments the ad got on their social media page.

I could go on and on about how different owners measure branding effectiveness. We can recount the old parable of the blind men and the elephant. For one person, the elephant is like a rope, for another it is like a tree trunk. We may end up making a similar mistake in how we measure our branding effectiveness.

The most astute brand marketers try and set up measuring metrics that cover all the elements mentioned earlier, but with clear-cut time markers. Some results of the branding efforts will have to be measured at short time intervals, some at longer ones. Some others will need an even longer time span for evaluation. We can call short-term measurement the **brand dashboard**. Medium-term brand performance measurement is **brand track**. Long-term branding effectiveness is **brand audit**.

i. *Brand Dashboard: A snapshot of brand health*

A brand dashboard, as the name indicates, is a data dashboard that a brand owner needs to have in front of them. Just as a dashboard on your car tells you the speed at which you are travelling, the fuel left in the tank, the engine temperature and other vital inputs, this daily dashboard measures your brand's performance. If you are a digital-first operation, like a web-based news service or a mobile app, you may actually have a 'live dashboard' that tracks usage by the minute or by the second. If you are a packaged foods' brand, you may want to create a monthly dashboard. It should reflect the sales of the brand, marketing inputs provided during the month and competitor activities. The monthly dashboard should also capture digital features like website visits, social media mentions, etc.

Sometimes, the digital efforts are run by the IT department and they operate in a different zone. In a large regulatory body that was doing a fair bit of consumer education advertising, we found that the website traffic was not monitored by the marketing communication team. Why? Simply because the website was being managed by the IT department.

A brand dashboard should capture all elements that are available. For instance, data on competitor's activities are available from various sources. Your own sales force is a great source of competitive intelligence. Advertising spends are tracked by various organisations. Why is this important to monitor on a daily basis?

Let us assume that your brand has been doing well and growing month on month. But in August, the sales dipped. What was the reason? Is it possible that a new competitor has entered? Or did an old competitor run a sales offer? Did one of the competitors increase their ad spends to absurd levels? Was there was a price cut? An environmental impact like a cyclone or flood? Did your product have a quality issue?

If all this sounds relevant only for a B2C company, hold on. In a B2B environment, too, you need a brand dashboard. Xerox pioneered the concept of the SPANCO selling model—suspect, prospect, approach, negotiate, close and order. At the end of every month, you not only measure the orders you landed but also the suspects, prospects, etc. One key metric they used in their selling was product demonstrations. They had worked out an algorithm that predicted that if you did over 100 demonstrations in January, this would lead to a sale of twenty copiers in the month of March (more about this in the chapter on selling and negotiation).

When I was running the Yellow Pages sales team which numbered seventy-five in New Delhi, we had a large white board on which the figures of ten teams, each with around eight members' achievements, was updated on a daily basis. We monitored both the number of orders/closures as well as the value of the order. This was in another era. Now, the same is done digitally: sitting in Mumbai, one can monitor sales efforts of a 1,000-member sales team through the use of smartphone-based apps like FieldAssist or Salesforce. Using AI, you can analyse the results in real time.

A brand dashboard is not too difficult to build and it will pull data from various databases at regular intervals. It is known that some large traditional Indian groups have the system of drawing up a daily balance sheet and profit-and-loss statement. A jeweller once mentioned that they always replace the gold they sell every day with new gold bought at the same price. The profit they make is therefore not determined by the fluctuations of gold prices. Sensible, I thought.

ii. Brand Track: Monitoring progress consistently

While the brand dashboard gives us a bird's eye view of brand performance in real time, we do need to dive deeper into brand health. This is done through what we call brand track. Here, not only do we depend on the data that is available from various syndicated sources but we may also have our own primary measurement of a few key metrics. B2C organisations monitor not just brand sales but also brand image parameters.

You have launched your new fabric softener with the fluffy kitten imagery. How is the image of this brand doing compared to the market leader, Comfort, across various attributes like softness, ease of use, value for money and so on? Is the brand moving upwards in the perception of consumers? I admit some amount of social media listening will help gauge the direction of consumer conversations, but in order to get a better view, you may need to interview around 500 to 1,000 consumers every month and see how they rate your brand. The kind of granular data collected randomly may not be available from social media posts.

Why is this important? If you have launched a new branding initiative, you may not be able to get any sale results for a few weeks, maybe even a few months, which may lead to the mistake of abandoning a good brand building effort too early. If you are able to run a comprehensive brand track at monthly or bi-monthly intervals, you will know if your brand scores are moving up. So while your sales may be slow, if your image scores are rising, your sales will also start climbing. But there is another side to this. If you are an incumbent brand and have a strong market presence, watch out. Your image scores often lag your sales, that is, your image may be slower to react to competitor pressures.

By and large, if you have set up a robust brand dashboard that gives you daily or weekly data and a brand track that checks your brand's health at regular intervals, maybe bi-monthly or quarterly, you are on your road to understanding how your branding efforts are working. Remember that these measurements are there to ensure that you continuously improve your return on marketing investments.

iii. Brand Audit: A brand health deep dive

Brand measurement has yet another important stage, and this is the brand audit. You have launched your new branding initiative and things are going well. The brand dashboard is showing great numbers, and your brand track is showing good progress. How do you ensure that you will not be hit below the belt?

A brand audit helps us pull ourselves out of our own rabbit hole and see how the overall environment is changing. We need to do a brand audit definitely once in two years, if not annually. In this, we review all the branding initiatives we have done—from brand communication and product formulation to pricing and distribution. Instead of just looking at our own product's category, we will broadly examine substitute and complementary products. If we are a cosmetic brand selling multiple products to women, we may be missing the potential offered by men's cosmetics. Or if we are marketing a water purifier, we may not notice the growing market for air purifiers.

A brand audit is always done by an independent agency. If it is done internally, it should be done by a team not involved in the brand. If not, it is worth hiring a consultant to do this for you. Yes, this may cost money, but there could be one thing, just one thing they unearth that may make it all the cost and effort worthwhile.

If you are in a big company—B2B or B2C—you need to use all these tools to monitor your brand's journey. What if you are a small company? Does all this matter at all? Why not just worry about sales and nothing more?

Sales are an important metric, but in the absence of other parameters, it could result in wrong decisions being taken. For instance, we may conclude that our brand is doing brilliantly because sales have been going up. But what if it's only because there was a temporary shortage of a competitor's product, or a health scare that drove up demand for our product? On a different note, our sales may be sluggish for many different reasons—a price offer or heavy promotional spends by a competitor.

All good marketing plans need a good measurement system to ensure that branding efforts are having the desired results. Remember: **if you can't measure it, you can't manage it.**

> 'It was an interesting challenge that you have to stay true to the brand ... and equally it's about adapting to categories and consumers.'
>
> —*Raka Sinha, International Brand Director, L'Oréal Paris*

5. Brand Expansion: Expanding the Use of the Potion

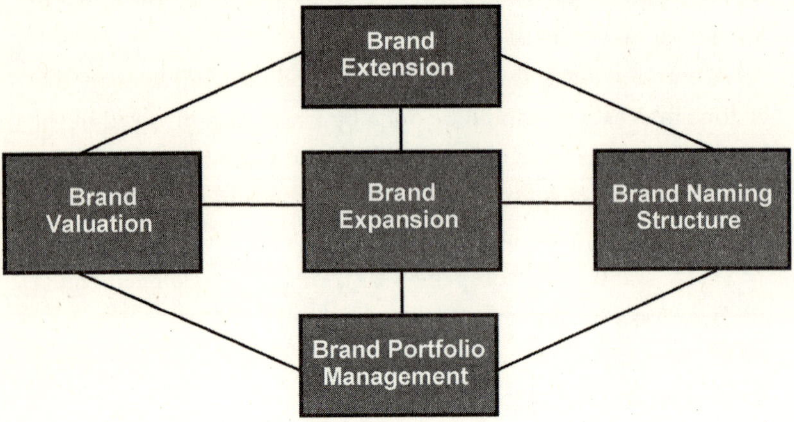

Brand expansion—developing a vision for the future of the company

Once a brand starts thriving, all companies desire to replicate this success by creating new brands. Let me give a few examples here.

'We have a floor shampoo for the institutional sector called FloClean. It's doing well. Now we want to launch a floor cleaner for the domestic segment. This will have a higher price than what we sell to institutions. Should we give it a different name?'

'Our upholstery brand is seen as premium. We have successfully launched bed linen under the same brand. But our sales team feels that our pricing is too high. Should we launch a lower-priced brand of bed linen?'

'We introduce twenty new models of cycles every year. While we have two primary brands, we also have numerous sub-brands. What is the right mix of brand-to-sub-brand hierarchy?'

All brands want to expand their footprint. On one level, with increasing competition, you cannot expect to sell the same product for years on end. You'd need to improve your product and introduce new features, just to stay competitive. So will you keep changing your brand? Or will you manage the changes within your primary brand?

It looks easy to build a second or third brand after you have tasted success once. But in an increasingly crowded world, launching successive brands is not going to be easy. But how do we handle the complexity as we introduce new products to new segments of consumers?

i. The importance of brand architecture

The first step is to understand that there has to be a kind of brand architecture you need to adopt. The simplest system is called the 'branded house' model. Using this model, all products are offered under the same name. A good Indian example is Amul. There is Amul milk, Amul chocolate, Amul ghee, Amul butter, Amul ice cream and so on (interestingly, when Amul ice cream was being launched, some experts opined that Amul, a housewife brand, would not be appealing to the youth/kids). The opposite end of the spectrum is the 'house of brands' model. The best example is Procter & Gamble, a corporation which literally invented the branding concept. So while P&G is the parent brand, it has multiple brands that it oversees, including Ariel, Head & Shoulders, Pampers, Pantene, Olay, Febreeze, etc. While these two are outstanding examples of two types of brand architecture, you have multiple hybrid models in the middle. Some companies use one brand for a set of products and an adaptation for another lot. Nestlé has milk and several product offerings under its primary brand, but it also has other brands like Nescafé and Nestum (which have a 'Nes' in their brand name) that offer a different set of products, along with independent brands like Milo and Maggi.

What is the right model for you? And how do you decide what you need to do?

One simple principle to follow is that the fewer brands you have, the better you will be able to use your resources. But you may also run the danger of damaging your main parent brand with an indiscreet new extension.

Expanding the range of products is the lifeblood of the branding dharma. You might need to launch new exciting offerings under your brand, just to continue your momentum. How do you name them?

ii. Offering new products as brand variants

The simplest way of handling new offerings is to treat them as variants. Nothing more. If your masala brand is called Raaja, then you will have Raaja Sambhar Masala, Raaja Chhole Masala and Raaja Pav Bhaji Masala. The parent brand remains prominent. If you want to do a little more than plain variant branding, you could add a little descriptor, like Raaja Trichy Sambhar Masala, Rajaa Royal Chhole Masala and Rajaa Chowpathy Pav Bhaji Masala. Remember you cannot start using the variant labelling as your new brand. You brand remains Raaja.

iii. Going forward with brand line extensions

The next thing you may want to do is offer line extensions. A line extension is a product that does a similar function as your parent product. A laser printer and an inkjet printer offer the same use, that is, printing, but under the Hewlett-Packard brand they are known simply by their line extension names of HP LaserJet and HP InkJet.

iv. Full stretch with brand extensions

Finally, you may want to take your brand across to a new product category that is relatively unconnected to your primary business—that is a brand extension. An upholstery brand may want to start manufacturing carpets; both belong to the décor industry but don't share any other common ground. A soap brand may want to enter the shampoo category, which is a different product but in the same industry of skincare or personal care.

When a brand tries to create a line or a brand extension, it is important to watch out for the collateral damage to the parent business, especially if the extensions are going to carry the same brand name. If the extension does well, everybody benefits. Sometimes, the extension can help the parent brand—a customer coming to buy a carpet may also buy new upholstery for their home. The flipside spells danger. If the extension fails, it will cost you money. But the bigger danger is that the extension may damage the parent brand. Your soap is a success, so you launch a shampoo under the same name, but this receives a very poor response for some reason. Perhaps it is not regarded as budget-friendly or consumers think it causes more hair fall. If you identify this early enough (with your brand dashboard, if I may add), you might be able to recall the product and bury it in your backyard. But if the word spreads, can you imagine the damage it will cause to your currently successful soap brand?

Does this mean that we should not experiment with brand extensions? By all means, we should. The first port of call should be dabbling in variants, that is, simply making a variety of offerings under the same brand name, for the same consumer. The next step is to look at line extension—same brand name, same or similar usage, same or different consumer. Finally, we have the more complicated brand extension where everything is different and new. One important filter to apply is the competency analysis your company has to make for the new product or service and the competitive pressures it will face. Just because you have achieved success in one domain does not mean you will be able to succeed in others.

Brand expansion is something all successful brands should undertake—but be cognisant of the process and the pitfalls. While you look at brand expansion, keep in mind a branding architecture model before you start on your journey—and be cautious. If you create too many brands, you might never have enough resources to support all of them.

6. Brand Magic Potion: The Process, The Results

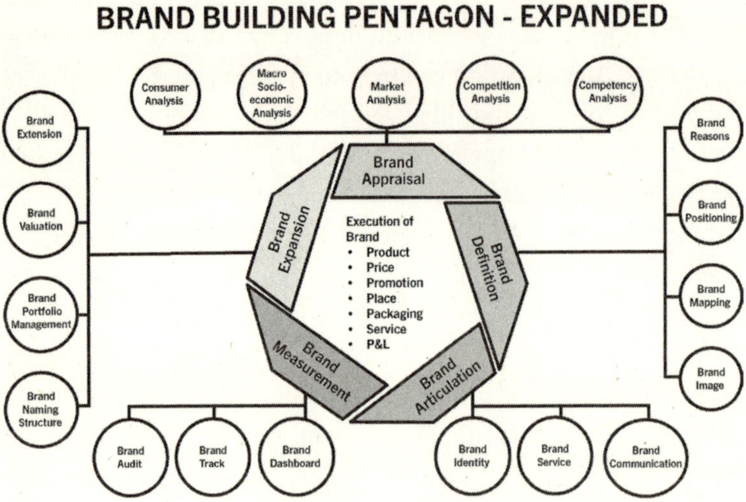

An expansion of the brand building pentagon

Whatever may be your current situation, you will benefit from applying the five-step process we have discussed here. Remember these simple steps: brand appraisal, brand definition, brand articulation, brand measurement and brand expansion.

Let us return to the four individuals we met at the beginning.

The masala manufacturer from Bhopal who wants to do branding. The start-up entrepreneurs who want to enter the kids' toy business. The B2B marketer who is not sure if branding will help him perform better. And the big company CEO who wants his marketing team to understand and use data more intelligently.

In all these cases, irrespective of size and scale, our five-step model of branding can help. For instance, the small entrepreneur from Bhopal would have less resources at his disposal, but his task is also simpler. He only needs to understand the city of Bhopal to start with—maybe he can do that through intense market visits. The B2B marketers also have a different task at hand. Their customers may only be a few dozen, but if they invest some effort in understanding them, they will be able to strengthen their brand and also mould their services to better suit client requirements.

Brand building is not a set of random acts but a process that needs to be followed rigorously. There is no guarantee that your brand will be an outstanding success just because you follow a good process. But chances are that the process will give you a good indication of the hurdles you will be facing and will dramatically improve your chances of success.

Some of what we discussed may sound too basic, but from my experience I find that companies tend to jump to conclusions before doing their homework. The usual complaint is that we don't have the time, resources, people, etc. But all these are excuses. Today, a lot of data is available for free. A lot of talent is available on tap. And if you know how to use AI-based tools, some of your initial work can be done in a matter of minutes and you can easily increase your chances of success.

Summing Up

To recap, don't start your branding journey before you have all the ingredients. Do a deep dive to understand the market, the consumer, the competition, your competency and the sociocultural environment. This applies equally to all companies across all product categories, big or small.

The second step is to define your brand. You need to find the gap in the market and the market in the gap. The ultimate result is to develop a robust BPS. Use consumer intelligence, consumer research and retail analysis to arrive at a sharp BPS. Bolster that with a good brand key or a brand map.

The third step is to develop a brand articulation platform. What is the brand name, the logo, the colours? What will be the brand communication plan? How will you integrate all elements of brand communication under a cohesive IMC strategy?

The brand is launched, but your work does not end. You need to put in place a good brand measurement system. This could be a daily dashboard, a monthly brand track and an annual audit. You cannot hold that measuring sales is sufficient and nothing else is needed. No, your sales numbers may be hiding more than what they reveal. So, dive deeper, simply because if you can't measure it, you cannot manage it.

Finally, you need to figure out how you want to expand your brand. Will it be simple variants or will you enter new lines, with line extensions, or will you go even wider with new product extensions? As you explore all these options, be aware of the positive and negative impact of these moves.

You're all set to start on a successful branding journey. You now know how to brew the brand magic potion in any category. Use it wisely, use it well.

Carpe diem.

> 'When you read up on any brand, you realise that there is so much diversity—a lot of things to be fixed. That is exciting.'
>
> —*Mayur Hola, Head of Global Brands, OYO Hotels*

3

The Wheel: Selling and Negotiation

Let us never negotiate out of fear; but let us never fear to negotiate.
—*John F. Kennedy*

Think of the following scenarios and imagine what you would do!

HR manager to the applicant: 'We think your education and your experience fits our requirements. And our interview panel feels you are right for the opening we have. But we will not be able to match your current pay package. You should know that we are a very reputed organisation. *This is a small sacrifice to join our group.*'

Broker to the prospective buyer: 'Sir, the seller has many offers lined up. But they will not go below ₹85 lakh. I know your budget is only ₹70 lakh. *What do you want me to tell them?*'

Purchase manager to vendor sales executive: 'Your product meets our specifications. And, as you know, we are a big buyer. But we will not be able to pay your asking price. Our offer is $1.5 per kilo. *That is the best we can offer!*'

Five-year-old kid to her mother: 'Mom, you promised I can get a toy, a book and a game. *I will not leave the shop till you allow me to buy all three!*'

Car sales executive to prospective buyer: 'This model of the car in silver grey is available for you right now. But there is a lot of demand. *You will have to make up your mind now.*'

These are some typical situations where you are getting pushed to take a decision. You are tempted to say 'yes' to the offer. You are getting that job, albeit at a lower pay grade. Or you are getting a big new customer but with some serious caveats.

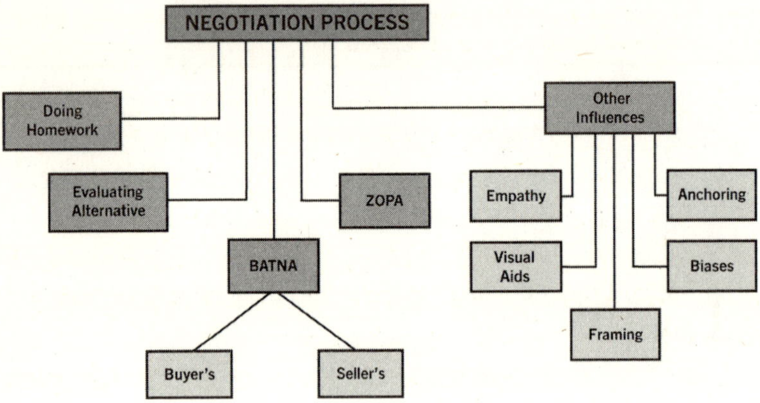

The many steps of negotiation planning

As my former boss once told me, 'If you can't walk away from a deal, **the deal owns you**.' And if you are not dispassionate about the deal, you will never be able to get to the right value for your offering—whether you are a buyer or a seller.

This chapter is a ride through the process of selling and negotiation and what it entails to get to a win-win position. **Remember, you can negotiate in any situation.** There is a branch in special forces that has experts who only do hostage negotiations. Even when you think your back is against the wall, you can negotiate a better deal. Maybe it will be a few extra days of paid leave or better credit terms or a 5 per cent cash discount. There is always some money on the table that you may be leaving behind if you don't negotiate.

This chapter will introduce you to the various sides of negotiations and the proven techniques that can help you when facing any of the situations mentioned earlier. Even if you have a kid throwing a tantrum, you can negotiate. One tip though: never ever take a kid shopping on an empty stomach!

Why Negotiate?

The first tenet we will look at is that negotiation is always an option. We often get scared to get into a negotiation. And if we are buying, we sometimes feel intimidated. How can we ask for a better price? There is also a niggling doubt that we will destroy our image if we negotiate. If we are selling, we are anxious to close the sale, and that shows in our behaviour or on our face.

Don't get me wrong. I will not negotiate with Ashok, my regular fruit vendor, or Raju the electrician. In fact, I often pay them a little more than their ask. I also know it is futile to negotiate in a store that has fixed prices on everything. Fortunately, not everything comes with a fixed price tag. But if we overcome our fear of negotiation, we can deliver a lot more value, for ourselves and for our companies.

As John F. Kennedy has so rightly observed, let us never be afraid to negotiate.

But why negotiate?

You may feel more comfortable not negotiating. It may be an attitudinal issue with you. If so, you need to get out of this zone. When you get into a negotiation, you have to remember that you will be spending precious time on it. What is the benefit you are hoping to gain? What is it going to cost, in terms of money and time? Is it going to be worth your while to negotiate? And as you begin negotiating, remember there is a risk and a reward. If you are expecting a very small reward, then evaluate the risk.

Imagine this: you work for this company that manufactures a spare part that goes into high-end automobiles. After much effort, your product has been cleared by the quality control department. The company wants to place a trial order. They are offering you a very low price which just about covers your variable cost. Should you negotiate a better price? By starting a negotiation process, what is the risk you will be running into? Will it antagonise the buyer? And what if the buyer is just floating a low-price balloon to test your conviction?

It is easy to accept the order and declare victory. But you should stop and think. If you accept the low price, then that may become the norm, and it will end up destroying value as far as your P&L is concerned. But if you seek a discussion, it might upset the buyer. And finally, who is the buyer, the purchase executive or the R&D person who cleared the product?

Negotiation need not be win-lose. It can be win-win. It can be even more than a win-win. The buyer gets a new source for an important part, and you get a new customer.

A good negotiation process consists of five steps: preparation, proposal, debate, bargaining and closing.

The most important step is probably preparation. What are you going to do before the negotiation even starts? What'll be your homework?

Doing Your Homework

In 1921, Theodore Roosevelt was running for the post of US presidency and the campaign was gathering steam. But the campaign manager had a problem. He had printed three million pamphlets with Roosevelt's photograph without seeking the permission of the copyright owner, the photographer. If the photographer were to get the pamphlet, a remote possibility, but a possibility nevertheless, he could sue the campaign for $1 per pamphlet, a total cost of $3,000,000. If the pamphlet was to be reprinted, that would cost $1 million. Two bad options indeed.

The campaign manager had a vital piece of information, something that the photographer did not have. He then sent a telegram to the photographer: 'We are planning to distribute millions of pamphlets with Roosevelt's picture on the cover. It will be great publicity for the studio whose photograph we will use. How much will you pay us to use yours? Respond immediately.'

The photographer fell into the trap and offered to pay $250 to get the photograph printed. What could have been a $3,000,000 blunder was turned around creatively.

What was at work here? Was it plain sleight of hand or something more?

In every negotiation situation, neither party has perfect information. There is what we call 'information asymmetry'. Each party is privy to their set of information. In the above case, the campaign manager knew that the pamphlet was already printed. The photographer did not have that information and did not realise that he was being played.

If you are getting ready to negotiate, you have to do your homework. And the first thing to do is to gather all the information you possibly can. Because in negotiation, information is king.

In the automotive spare parts story we looked at earlier, you may be getting played if you did not know the price being paid by the company to its current vendor or if that vendor was having delivery issues. If you do have that information, or even an indication of that, you are in a better situation. Remember, the buyers may have done their homework. They may know that you are supplying an identical spare part to their competitor at a particular price. So, not only should you be collecting the relevant information to bolster your arguments but you should also know what information the buyers may have at their disposal.

If we go back to the interviewer offering you a salary package that is lower than what you are getting—you can say yes. But you can also ask for time and then do your homework. What is the company paying other people with your level of skills and experience? What is the promotion policy of the company? When will they give you your next increment? By knowing more, you will be able to take a better call on what you should do. It is possible that you accept the offer but indicate some caveats, 'Madam, I am happy to accept your offer since it has been a long-term dream to work in your group. But the salary seems a little confusing. I know a few people of my experience profile who are getting much more. Will I be able to catch up, if I do well, in the next two years?'

Never get into a negotiation if you have not done your homework. And don't try to bluff your way through the negotiation. You will be caught out. If you have not done your homework, you will end up cutting a sorry figure when the other side points out the flaws in your argument.

What do you do if you have not collected the information required? Simple. Ask for time. Ask for a day or two. Even a week.

Then spend the time collecting information that can prepare you for some serious negotiation. Successful negotiation starts with better preparation. Without the right information, your negotiation will crumble in a few minutes. If you have not done your preparation, either ask for time, or dumbly accept the offer. And be ready to find that offer getting sliced further. More about thin slicing later.

How do I collect information and how do I evaluate the options when doing so? These are likely to be your next questions. We will jump into the area of evaluation of alternatives next.

> 'How you manage your down will determine how up you go.'
>
> *—Raka Sinha, International Brand Director, L'Oréal Paris*

Evaluating Alternatives

Imagine that you have a car you need to sell. It is now ten years old and has given you good service. But now you want to sell it and maybe buy a new one that better suits your changed requirements.

What information will you look for and what are the alternatives?

You bought the car for ₹15 lakh and have maintained it well. No one else has driven it. Looking at car comparison sites, you know that a car of a similar vintage is available for ₹5 lakh.

In *Getting to Yes,* Roger Fisher and Willian Ury of Harvard University coined the term BATNA (Best Alternative To a Negotiated Agreement). Let's say you have a cousin who loves your car but can only offer you ₹4.5 lakh. That is your BATNA, since you can get that price without any lengthy negotiations.

You are aware that the price (₹5 lakh) that is quoted in the public domain is a general figure. A lot depends on the specific conditions of the car; you want to see if you will get at least ₹5.5 lakh. This is your 'reservation price' (RP). Ideally, you want a bit more for your car, and your 'stretch price' (SP) is ₹7 lakh.

You have a good range now. But are you ready to sell? Not yet. If you are to do a good job of negotiating, you need to view this from the other side as well.

So let's switch sides. You are in the market for a second-hand car. Your neighbour has an old one that you can buy for ₹4 lakh but you want to look at options. You have checked out some sources and know that most second-hand cars are available for ₹5 lakh. Depending on the condition of the car, you are willing to pay a little more, maybe ₹6 lakh. Given a choice, you would like to clinch the deal for ₹4 lakh. Your range is therefore clear (₹4–6 lakh).

The seller's BATNA is ₹4.5 lakh, RP is ₹5.5 lakh and SP is ₹7 lakh.

The buyer's BATNA is ₹4 lakh, RP is ₹5 lakh and SP is ₹6 lakh.

Look how this is mapping out below:

	BATNA	RP	SP
Seller	4.5	5.5	7.0
Buyer	4.0	5.0	6.0

You have the buyer's and seller's BATNA and RP. Between these two, you get the zone of possible agreements (ZOPA). In this case, the ZOPA is between ₹4.5 lakh and ₹6 lakh. Anything in the middle of this range is a win-win for both the buyer and seller.

This is an ideal situation where you know both parties' BATNA and RP. In reality, you will not have at your disposal all elements of information and alternatives. But if you make the effort, you can piece together some more info and be ready for some serious negotiation.

If we go back to the automotive spare parts vendor example, your BATNA will be the price you are offering other customers. You can, at any time, sell the component to the other party. And your RP may be 10 per cent more.

Often, we just stop with this bit of analysis, but it is not enough to get your BATNA and RP on paper. You have to make the effort to find out the buyer's BATNA and RP. Even if this is an approximation, it is important to get this information.

Let us now try and learn some techniques useful in negotiations.

The Anchoring Effect

Let us consider a different situation and see how principles of negotiation can be applied to that: the situation is buying an apartment. You can find out what the seller had originally paid for the flat and the price of the last deal in the same or nearby building.

You have done your homework and worked out all the alternatives. Where do you start? Who should go first?

If you are going to buy the apartment and you want to set a low bar, you can open the discussion by saying, 'We love the apartment. But we cannot pay more than ₹60 lakh!' You did not wait for the seller to name their price, which you were sure would be ₹90 lakh or ₹95 lakh.

By going first and giving a number, you are trying to create an anchor for the negotiation process, in this case, ₹60 lakh. The seller has registered this price as a marker and has to work upwards. You are happy with that, since your RP is ₹70 lakh.

Alternatively, the seller may go first and say, 'I have an offer for ₹85 lakh and I am not interested in anything less than ₹90 lakh.' The seller has beat you to it. Now ₹85–90 lakh is the anchor.

Why does this work? That's because anchoring is a strong force. Psychologists have run experiments where a random number, brought to the attention of the subject, influences their assessment by creating its own anchoring effect. For example, if I project a number, such as 900, and then ask a random question like, 'How many people died of COVID-19?' I may get one number. If I project another number, such as 10,00,000, and ask the same question, I will probably get a much higher answer, because the anchor is much higher.

In many buying–selling situations, the buyer or seller may name a number that is artificially too low or too high. What do you do if you are caught on the wrong foot? One option is to take it up from there knowing that the anchoring effect may cause its own problems. Another option is to ignore the high or low number indicated and assume that you are making the first offer.

A simple rule of thumb if you are buying something of rather indeterminate value is to ask the seller for their asking price.

However, if you have done your homework and have worked out the alternatives, go first and indicate a number.

Anchoring is a strong source of creating a bias. But that is not the only bias you need to be wary of.

How to Overcome Biases

We saw how one party in a negotiation can go first and create an 'anchoring effect'. This is a source of bias. This can come in many forms.

Buying and selling a home is a highly orchestrated affair in many parts of the world. In many countries, selling a home requires a good real estate agent. The agent asks the client to move out of the home for a few days and 'dresses up' the house by hiring some new furniture, changing the curtains and upholstery and displaying some nice books and flowers. In addition to these subtle cues, the agent may even bake some cookies for the open house when prospective buyers start trooping in.

Let us look at the various biases at work here. For one, the seller and the buyer never meet face to face till the deal value is agreed upon between the two parties through the real estate agent. Why, you may ask? By avoiding this face-to-face meeting, you are taking out one element of the bias: 'We have lived here for twenty years and love the place' or 'We are a newly married couple, you will make us so happy if you sell it to us'. By dressing up the place, the buyer gets a biased view of the home. The cookie magic is yet another interesting biasing device. A home with the aroma of freshly baked cookies not only smells good but also looks and feels better. There is a multiplicity of biases at work here.

The house will never look so pretty when people start living in it. The smell may not be anywhere near that of a freshly baked cookie. And so on.

Remember, the person who is negotiating with you will be trying to create these biases to work in their favour. Offering a cup of tea and cookies helps create a bias. Not offering coffee or tea creates a different kind of pressure on the visitor.

Some biases are created by the other party. Others are self-created.

If you consider the job-hunting situation, prospective candidates tend to overemphasise on the more vivid features of the job. That is called a vividness bias. A candidate may pay too much attention to features that stand out, ignoring the less visible ones. I remember advising a colleague who was getting an offer from a leading consumer packaged goods company. A thousand horses could not have stopped her since she thought that jumping from an advertising job in a client servicing role to that of an assistant brand manager was indeed a big leap. She had not realised what the next step would be and whether she would, some day in the future, be equated (in career terms) with a person who had joined that company from campus. The sheer charm of moving from advertising to a client job was so vivid that she did not realise that she was suffering from a severe case of vividness bias.

This bias is an entirely self-created trap. We are so excited about getting the offer or the order that we don't realise we may be making some vital mistakes.

On the other side, there might be the problem of egocentrism, overconfidence, irrational optimism and a sense of superiority—we may fail to realise that we are being biased. It helps to have a neutral person call out the biases. Thanks to my advice, my young colleague overcame the vividness bias and returned to the consumer packaged goods company to have a detailed discussion about her career path. It turned out that the HR executive could place her in a different position that would give her a better career trajectory. She ended up joining the company and moved to London a few years later.

In a corporate situation, there is a good exercise that can be used to climb out of a biased mindset. A CEO wanted consensus on a new project. Half of his management committee members supported the project, but the others were dead against it. He decided to give them a thought experiment, and told the supporters to work together for an hour and come back with arguments against the project. Then he told the opposing team members to come back to the management committee with arguments that favoured the project. And a couple of hours later, he had an agreement from all of them. This is called the 'arguing for and arguing against' technique. You could try it at home when your kids are fighting over which programme to watch on TV.

We sometimes use words that end up influencing the other party. Let us assume that you have to conclude a long negotiation process to sell some spare parts to an automobile major. As you close the discussion, you say, 'By the way, we can start supplying immediately.' In saying 'By the way', you have taken away the importance of this offer and the other party is left with the prejudiced impression that you came ill-prepared to the negotiation. Phrases that sound tentative like 'by the way', 'possibly', 'maybe' tend to cause a negative bias towards your offer.

Your own negotiation style can create a bias. There are five broad styles that books tell us about:

- Assertive, meeting your own goals at the expense of others.
- Collaborative, looking for joint gains and finding ways to expand the scope.
- Compromising, taking a little less and settling quickly.
- Avoidant, failing to meet any goal.
- Accommodating, listening a lot more and giving up a lot to reach the goal.

In addition, biases can be created by your voice. If you are with a buyer who is soft-spoken, be aware that your voice may sound too loud. The same may be okay in front of a boisterous buyer.

The field of behavioural economics gives us yet another area where we get blindsided. The concept of 'prospect theory' which got Daniel Kahneman his Nobel Prize is all about how we believe what we have is of greater value than what the market may ascribe to it. Multiple experiments have shown that we suffer from what is called 'loss aversion'. We hate to lose something that we have, even if we know it is not of great value. So we think our house should fetch a better price than an identical home in the next building. We think our car should get a better price since we looked after it so well. In reality, this is simply because of the loss aversion phenomenon. As the saying in Tamil goes, '*Kakaiku than kunju pon kunju*' (A crow thinks its chick is golden.)

Using Visual Aids and Decision Trees

Years ago, when I was in advertising, we headed out for a negotiation discussion with one of our large clients. We did not expect fireworks and were rather well-prepared.

This client worked with our agency on a fee basis. To explain, most advertising agencies work with clients on two broad systems. The old traditional way of compensating the agency was through media commission, as in we create an ad that runs on TV and we get 15 per cent of the media spends. The other system is based on 'fees'. The client estimates the kind of work to be done. The agency works out the number of hours or days needed to deliver the jobs, through the year. A detailed calculation of the kind of teams, their cost to company and an agency margin is worked out and agreed upon with the client. This annual cost is then paid by the client in twelve instalments.

This client had been working with the agency on a fee basis. The fee had been unchanged for two years since the company was going through some challenging times. From the agency side, we had been giving them great service and many senior managers were involved. But now our fee was definitely in need of a generous upward revision.

In a situation like this, it is always better to prepare the ground. Never get into a fee negotiation cold. It can backfire badly. On our part, we had been making polite noises over three months that our fee was in need of a revision. Fortunately, business for the client was picking up and there was much to be celebrated.

We could have thrown in a number, say a 20 per cent increase, and the client may have agreed with some haggling. But we decided to do it more professionally with some visual aids.

The team on the account was asked to catalogue all the work done, both released and unreleased (a lot of work an ad agency creates ends up in the drawers of the creative directors, especially if the client has a large team that loves to make changes). Then detailed manpower estimates were drawn up: the teams that worked on the account, the time allocated, the cost of the talent. We had also estimated the media spends of the client so that we could draw a simple 'fee versus media commission' argument. All this analysis told us that our fee needed an upward revision of at least 35 per cent. Were we asking for too much? We decided to dig and find out what other companies of a similar nature were paying their clients. Doing so confirmed our hunch.

We walked in to the client office and were ushered into the CMO's cabin. We requested that we adjourn to the conference room for a presentation. 'What, you guys want to make a presentation on the fee you want?' asked the CMO, incredulous. 'Give us thirty minutes, sir, to present some details to you,' chipped in the smiling client services director from our agency who was running the account.

What followed was an engrossing presentation that took the CMO through the agency's ad history. How much work had been produced over the last two years; the teams that had worked on the account; the numerous consumer insight mining projects undertaken. And more.

The fee request was in the last two slides of this thirty-slide presentation. I don't have to tell you that we got our request okayed.

The next time you are getting ready to negotiate a new contract, a new deal, don't underestimate the importance of visual aids.

To start with, you should use decision trees to figure out the various options that you need to examine. For instance, one of the decision tree's branches we had in the above case was a simple increase in the fees as per our estimate of time used to service the account. Another branch had no fee increase but a reduction in the services offered. We could charge extra for all the artworks created or for the consumer research the agency did on a routine basis. The idea is to create multiple branches in the decision tree, then evaluate the pros and cons of each branch from the point of view of profitability as well as implementation hassles. We could have a decision tree option that said we will work on the same fee but estimate and bill for the strategic planning and consumer research separately.

A decision tree analysis can help you examine all the options and assign weightages to each of them. What if the client said no? What will we do next? What are the options?

For instance, if you are looking at a job switch, you may have multiple options that cover the salary package, incentives, perquisites like house/car, opportunities to attend international conferences, location of office, relocation expenses, medical insurance and even opportunities for being sponsored for management development programmes. You need to plot all the options and then create a decision tree to help you see the options.

Power of Framing and Reframing

There is this wonderful little tale about the power of reframing

A young monk liked an occasional smoke (to those of you who are a little aghast, even Swami Vivekananda enjoyed the occasional cigarette; this story has nothing to do with the great Swamiji though). Our young man was in a monastery where young monks were being groomed for their future duties. Many hours were to be spent on meditation and prayer.

The monk went up to the head of the monastery with a request: 'Sir, may I smoke when I am praying?'

'Absolutely not! Don't you know prayer is a solitary task. How can you pollute it with smoke?' replied the head monk promptly.

If you were the young monk, what would you have done? How would the power of reframing help you? Here is a suggestion. The monk might have tried phrasing his request this way instead: 'Sir, may I pray when I am smoking?' The answer to this may have been: 'Of course. There is always time and place for prayer. It is good to know that you are thinking of praying when you are smoking.'

That is the power of reframing. Presented in one frame, the request sounds preposterous. But when reframed, it sounds perfectly reasonable.

Here is an example from my life as a brand consultant.

We were invited to work on a competitive strategy project by one of the most respected multinational companies in India. After a few rounds of discussion, the client was convinced that the competitive strategy process we had was indeed unique and could lead to some interesting insights. Through the discussions, we had convinced the client that the entire process could take around ten to twelve weeks since it involved hundreds of interviews, literature review covering decades of published material, etc. We also promised the client that the most senior executives of the consulting division team would work on the project. Then it came to discussing the cost of the project. The figure we quoted, with all the above rationale, seemed a little on the higher side to the client manager who was negotiating with us. It was then that I decided to do the monk experiment and reframe the cost. I asked, quite innocently, how many ad films the company made every year. The manager did not understand the relevance of the question but replied that it was around ten. I complimented him for the wonderful quality of the films the company had commissioned. The client manager was pleased. Then I reframed my offer: 'This project, which may result in unearthing several business opportunities and threats, will cost you as much as one of those ten films. So look at it this way—instead of making ten films this year, make nine.'

Needless to say, the project estimate was cleared.

It is said that good negotiators are problem solvers at heart. They find interesting new ways of solving their problems as well as those of the negotiating party. In this case, we were able to build an argument for the client manager to take it up with their CEO and CFO when asked why the cost was so high. Remember that reframing the offer can help both parties.

Techniques, Tactics and Paradigms

John Nash won the Nobel Prize in 1994 in mathematics for his work on game theory. The Hollywood film *A Beautiful Mind* presented the challenges he faced on his quest for the truth. In fact, there is a connection between negotiation success and Nash. It was Nash who mathematically proved the Swiss philosopher Jean-Jaques Rousseau's view that when opposing teams collaborate, the pie almost always expands in size. Each party ends up getting more. I believe this is even better than win-win, since each party gets more than what they bargained for.

How does this 'expanding the pie' paradigm work in real life?

In my book *Spring: Bouncing Back from Rejection*, I narrate an anecdote involving a mom and two kids who are fighting over who will get the bigger slice of the pizza. One way of managing this battle is to get one kid to cut the pizza and let the other kid get the first choice. A better way might be to find out what each of the kids love. Maybe one kid likes the centre of the pizza while the other kid likes the crust. So, instead of cutting the pizza in half, you could cut it into two circles—one for the kid who likes the centre, one for the kid who likes the crust.

In a business situation, companies can examine how they can expand the pie. Buyers often start by tabling a price they are willing to pay for an annual contract. The seller can expand the pie with a better price, if the contract is for three years. The seller, by expanding the pie, has helped both parties get more out of the contract.

Let us call this the pie expansion technique.

As a part of the fifty-year celebration of our ad agency group, we wanted to organise a series of branding workshops in cities like Mumbai, Delhi, Bangalore and Chennai. Faculty cost was zero since all the sessions would be held by senior managers from the agency, but organising these workshops in a five-star hotel would cost a bomb. We wanted to keep the cost low, since 50 per cent of the participants would be from our own agency. The other attendants were to be executives from client organisations. Naturally, five-star prices were a stumbling block. Who would be interested in hosting us?

Fortunately, we found that one of the business schools in central Mumbai had a wonderful conference room. They wanted to get corporates to visit their campus and their glitzy new facility, and were willing to offer the facilities for free and even throw in lunch at reduced cost. They had a request. Could we allow five of their faculty to attend the workshop? We happily agreed and repeated the workshop on their Bangalore campus.

What did we do? We traded items that had different value to each of us. What was virtually no cost to us was seen as valuable by the business school. What we needed, a conference room, was an under-utilised facility for them. Trading items of unequal value can create great advantage for both parties.

You are in need of a new pair of glasses. You walk into an optician's store and examine the many frames on display. You really like one of them. The sales guy says the frame is from Italy and arrived the previous week. You want to know the price. He has managed to set the right expectations and says, 'Sir, it will be thirty-five thousand rupees.' You nod. The sales guy then says, 'The new polychromatic lenses will cost five thousand rupees.' You nod. He adds, 'Per lens.' (That is a cheeky attempt. I don't think any optician will do that.)

The sales guy has tried to thin-slice the price. He has gleaned your interest in the product and senses a definite 'buy' signal.

In an equipment sales situation, the seller may decide to sell just the equipment for an attractive price and add the service contract as an extra. Some car brands do not offer any free service, thin-slicing the cost of ownership.

Use this technique with care, lest you overdo it.

While negotiating, you may just want to get an entry. This is the FITD strategy. Foot in the door. You desperately want a trial order. You hope that by making the entry, you will be able to build your business from there. In behavioural economics, it is said that when you ask someone for a small favour, they tend to say yes. Once they have said yes to a small favour, they are ready to undertake bigger tasks for you. In a buying situation too, a buyer may be ready to give a small order, on a trial basis. Sometimes the seller, in their anxiety to get the order, bids too low a price. So even when a bigger order comes later, they end up not making much profit from the sale.

The opposite technique to FITD is the DIYF, or door in your face. Here, you make a big demand knowing that it will get rejected. Once it is rejected, remorse sets in and the other party may be in a mood for a softer deal. I remember negotiating with an ad filmmaker on two changes to be made to the film, knowing fully well that she would protest any changes at all since it would cost them money. So, instead of asking for just two changes, I asked for six. This kicked up a storm. But I ended up getting the two important changes I wanted.

Creating a powerful negotiating team is yet another technique that corporates use. In the team, there are clearly defined roles for the members. One person is the captain. The second one usually plays hardball—the tough nut to crack. Another is a Mr Nice Guy who makes all the polite sounds. The fourth member is the logical person who has all the numbers and the logic. It is ideal that your team has at least these four members.

While negotiating, beware of the winner's curse. This term became popular in the US after financial analysts showed that, more often than not, the company that acquires another after a bidding war ends up the loser (the acquisition becomes a big drain on the company). So winning a bidding war may, in fact, be a curse. The same is true of any negotiation. You may end up giving away too much to win a contract and let the competition have the last laugh.

Finally, as your negotiation winds to a close, don't forget to put everything in writing. As the old Chinese saying goes: 'The palest ink is better than the best memory.'

The Power of Empathy

A diversified corporation had a small business that made leather products for exports. The business was very steady and profits good. PST, the person looking after the business, also had other responsibilities. In one management committee meeting, attention drifted towards the leather business. The CEO wanted to know how it was doing and what the prospects were for the coming year. PST had done his homework and confirmed that orders were in place and the year should go well.

One of the other management committee members asked, 'How many customers do we have?'

PST replied that the unit dealt with just one customer who was based in Italy.

'Just one customer?' was the next question. To which the answer was, 'Yes, one customer who has been a great one to have for the last ten years.'

The discussion was getting more heated as other management committee members jumped in: 'Just one customer? They must be taking us for a ride!' and 'How are you sure you are getting the right price?' and 'If the customer knows you are totally dependent on them, they will take advantage of this vulnerability, no?'

PST was getting agitated. He decided to put an end to this discussion. He asked what the committee wanted from his business unit. Did they want it shut down? No, it was very profitable. Did they want him to expand the customer base? No, there was limitation in capacity.

'Can you get a price increase?' This was the final gauntlet flung at PST.

'Yes, most definitely,' replied PST bravely.

At the next quarterly meeting, PST proudly announced that the buyer had given him a 20 per cent price increase.

How did that happen? What technique did PST use? BATNA? ZOPA?

Well, none of the above. PST met the customer once a year. And this year when he met the customer in Italy, he politely asked if he could get a price increase. The buyer was surprised. Is the price not good enough? No, but the managing committee wanted to know if the buyer was happy enough to offer a price increase. The buyer knew that his vendor was not a faceless corporation, but PST, a loyal friend and supporter. How much would be good? PST suggested 15 per cent. The buyer said that he would make it 20 per cent. And that was the negotiation that never really happened.

If you think that is just fiction, let me assure you that this story is based on a real incident and one that demonstrates the power of empathy in negotiation. PST did not use any technique but successfully got a price increase because he had created a great deal of empathy with his customer. His customer did not want PST to lose face in front of the management committee.

Creating empathy is as simple as that. And it can work miracles.

While getting into a negotiation situation, we cannot ignore the importance of non-verbal cues.

To start with, when we enter a negotiation room or conference room, we need to read the room. If the buying party is sitting on one side, you can make out who is going to be the key negotiator, who is going to play a supporting role and who will be the hard bargainer.

As negotiation starts, you have to read the body language of the other side. Are their hands on the table? Or are their arms folded? Are they leaning forward or relaxing in the chair? Hands on the table, leaning forward is a positive. Leaning back with arms folded means things are not going well.

Finally, read the signals. In some negotiations, you end up speaking so much that you don't listen to the buying signals. If you are a car sales executive and extolling the many virtues of the vehicle, you may miss the fact that the customer asked about the delivery schedule. That, in sales language, is a 'buying signal'. By ignoring it, you are losing an opportunity to close the sale then and there. 'We received five cars of this model yesterday. We can deliver a car of your choice tomorrow,' may clinch the sale.

Also, do not ignore the softer aspects of negotiation. Remember that negotiation is between two people, two human beings. Studies have shown that adversarial negotiators close just about half the deals made by a cooperative, problem-solving negotiator. And often they get a lot less too.

The truth is unless you connect with the people you are negotiating with, you will not be able to make the deal. And even if you do, it will not be a good deal or it may not last the full distance. So even if you don't like the other party, you have to learn to accept them for what they are. Make that important human connection.

Negotiations with Children

Emperor Akbar was livid. Birbal was late. Akbar thundered, 'Birbal, this is the third time this week that you are late to this court. You know I cannot be kept waiting. You better have a good excuse to save your head!'

'My apologies, lord. My wife has gone to visit her mother,' replied Birbal.

'What do your wife's travels have to do with your arrival in my court, Birbal?' asked Akbar.

'Well, my lord, I was left with my five year old son and he delayed my departure.'

'What, delayed by your son! You expect me to believe that? Nonsense. How can an advisor to the most powerful kingdom in the world be hindered by a five-year-old?'

'My lord, my son kept making demands and I could not reach a settlement with him.'

'What, you negotiate with kings and ministers, and you could not negotiate with a five-year-old!?'

'My lord, if you don't believe me, let me enact it in front of you. Please humour me and play the role of the father. I will play the role of my son.'

Akbar was not sure where this was going but his anger did not come in the way of his good humour.

'Okay, Birbal. Let us play this game. And be ready for a severe penalty if you lose.'

'Yes, of course, my lord,' was Birbal's instant reply.

The game began.

'Papa, before you go to the king's court, you should get me the juiciest mango.'

Aha, that is easy, thought Akbar, and ordered his courtiers to get him a nice juicy mango.

'Here is the mango, my son. Now can I leave?'

'Thank you, Papa, but can you make it into a juice?' Akbar was quick to ask a courtier to take the mango from the son, Birbal, and make a glass of mango juice out of it.

'Here you are, my son. Now may I go?'

'Papa, thank you. But I have changed my mind. I want the mango!'

Akbar ordered his courtier to quickly bring another mango.

'Here is the mango, my son.'

'Papa, I want the same mango you showed me the first time.'

'But that was made into a juice, my son. Take this fresh mango!'

'No, Papa, I want the same mango!'

Akbar realised that it was not easy to negotiate with a child. He smiled and told Birbal to go home and play with his child for the day.

This story, a modified version of the original Akbar and Birbal story, is useful for demonstrating the difficulty of negotiating with children. The degree of difficulty is even higher because we tend to treat children differently from adults, regarding them as petty, temperamental and confused.

Negotiating with children can be fruitful when you take their concerns seriously without mocking them, and listen to them actively. How often have you heard a child tell their mother, 'You are not listening to me!' Listen to them with all your senses.

Try role reversal with them. 'If mommy didn't brush her teeth, would you be okay with that? Won't you be worried about mommy's teeth?'

Try communicating with them as clearly as possible. 'Don't you know your dad loves you a lot? So would dad make you do something that is not good for you?'

Focus on the goals without getting emotional. 'We agreed that you will go to sleep at nine o'clock so that you can get up in time for school. That was the agreement. Are you going to break that?'

In reality, you can change the behaviour of children by using the same negotiating techniques you use with adults. You can create a new frame, expand the scope of the discussion. 'You can't eat the chocolate right now, but if you eat an orange today, I'll give you the chocolate tomorrow.' Or try the incrementalism; thin slicing. 'Okay, you can read till nine-fifteen today. But tomorrow, you will go to bed at nine o'clock. Deal?'

When negotiating with children, try and visualise what is going through their mind. Try and listen to them carefully. Communicate honestly. Consult them at the right time. Be ready to trade items of different value with them. Most importantly, treat them with respect.

> 'Get into details. Speak to your customer. Know your data. Go to market. Do a cycle of sales. Marketing will then be much smoother.'
>
> —*Virat Khullar, Group Head, Marketing, Hyundai India*

Selling Skills

Negotiation is a key part of what we call selling skills. In marketing, you need to be good at selling. You are selling your product to your prospect. You are selling your ideas inside your company. You are selling ideas all the time. Many of the things we spoke about in the context of negotiation apply greatly to selling.

No sale can happen if you don't know who you are selling to and the mindset of the buyer. Xerox, once a much-revered B2B company, had a system called professional selling skills (PSS). Everyone in the sales and marketing team had to sit through a five-day training session every year. Every year! Why? The company was convinced that good selling practices tend to get eroded over time—even the best salespersons have to go through the PSS bootcamp. Pretty much like a team that goes into a coaching camp before a world cup tournament.

PSS categorised the sales process and customers in different stages, like a ladder—the SPANCO model, which I touched upon briefly earlier.

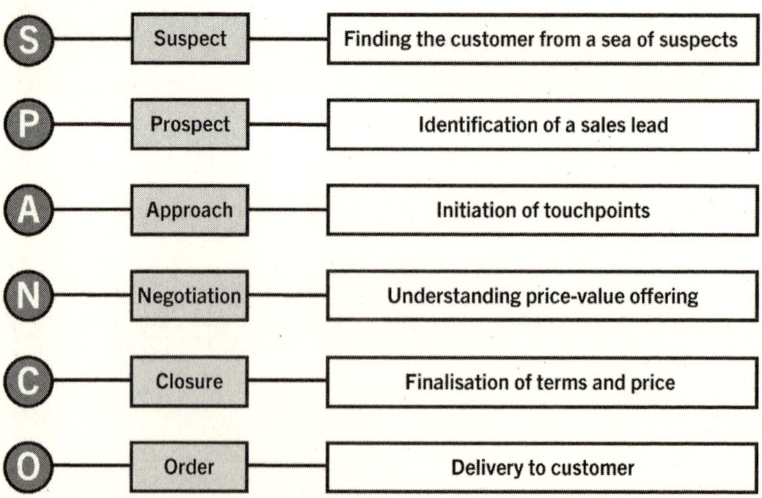

The SPANCO model

When you first approach a potential customer, they are a **suspect**. You don't know if they are interested unless they have sent you a request for information. Approaching an unknown customer is what we call 'cold calling'. The customer is a suspect and you have to do some homework before calling on them. The minimum you can do is to study their website or the LinkedIn profile of the person you are meeting.

At the next stage, when you have found out more about a suspect and you detect a potential sale, the suspect becomes a **prospect**. In order to convert a suspect into a prospect, you will have to use probing techniques that we will look into in a bit.

You have found out more about the customer and there is a prospect of a sale. You now help the customer understand more about what you are trying to sell. This is the **approach** stage. The customer will expect you to explain why they should buy your product and also analyse the merits and demerits of your product.

Often a sale is lost at the approach stage. If we are not able to answer the questions, the prospect loses interest and won't become a viable customer.

If you have managed to transition to the approach stage, the next stage is **negotiation**—a vital stage that we have analysed in detail earlier. This is followed by **closure**, and finally there is the **order**, where the prospect becomes a customer. A number of sales have been lost even at this last stage. A good salesperson is careful about understanding which stage a customer has reached and what can be done to get them to place the order. You push too hard, and you can lose the order. If you don't push at all, you may lose the order to a competitor who has something extra to sell.

In order to get a suspect to become a prospect, and then finally getting an order, you need to be master of all selling techniques. In very simple terms, selling is all about probing > supporting > closing.

You need to probe the suspect to find out the exact pain points that your product or service can solve. Probing can be open-ended or close-ended. In general, if the suspect is ready to speak, you can adopt an open-ended approach. For instance, if you are marketing photocopy machines and are speaking with the admin manager: 'How do you get photocopies done in your office?' (this is an open-ended probe). If the suspect is not willing to speak much, you may have to do a close-ended approach: 'Do you have photocopy machines in the office or do you use an outside service?'

By probing, you find out more about the customer. What are the pain points? What are they looking for? Then you get to the next stage of selling, which is to support. Here, you answer any concerns or questions that have come up. If the probing threw up price per copy as a pain point: 'Our copier can deliver up to 1,000 copies for a cost of less than 50 paisa per copy.'

Once you have supported the question well, you then move to close the order.

As you go through these stages, all that we saw about negotiation will apply. You need to be empathetic with your customer. Know their limits and constraints. You have to define your own BATNA and have a clear ZOPA. In the end, selling should be an enjoyable process for both the seller and the buyer. The seller will derive monetary benefits from the sale. The buyer obviously will derive greater value than the price paid. It is sometimes a dance that you have to carefully orchestrate. As you get better at this, you will be able to figure out what technique will work with which prospect, and you will become a champion salesperson.

> 'Never lose an opportunity to interact with a customer at any stage. Doing thirty [sales] calls a day has taught me more about the tea business than all the rules written on tea business.'
>
> *—Sunder Madakshira, Head of Marketing, Adobe India*

Consumer Packaged Goods/Durables: Sales Organisation

The world of selling, as far as consumer products and durables, is undergoing a tremendous flux. Many small direct-to-consumer brands have been built by using the power of e-commerce platforms, completely bypassing traditional general stores. The bigger companies have set up separate verticals in their sales organisation to handle general trade, modern trade and e-commerce.

In yesteryears, most companies had no choice but to set up an elaborate sales system to ensure that their product reached the large number of general trade (GT) outlets. The sales organisation used to consist of several hundred sales executives who called on forty-odd GT outlets a day in what was known as a planned journey cycle. They, in turn, reported to territory managers, who reported to regional managers. It was a well-oiled system and served the consumer packaged goods brands very well.

The emergence of modern trade (MT) over the last two decades has made bigger brands wake up to the different opportunity. Many of them have separate teams handling MT. Finally, the growth of e-commerce (and now quick commerce) has created its own requirement for sales support and service.

The pharma industry continues to operate with a large medical representative field force that calls on doctors and chemists in a fixed routine. The durables industry, too, has its own sales organisation that handles old-school durable outlets as well as the newer organised durables dealer channels.

Depending on the industry you are working in, there will be a sales organisation that will work well for you. The more visionary companies like Asian Paints have managed to steal a march over their competitors by focusing on building a robust sales system that could meet the requirements of the customers and the dealers.

Final Negotiations

As John F. Kennedy observed, we cannot be afraid to negotiate. We cannot see negotiation either as a cheap trick, nor should we be scared. A good negotiator sees an opportunity to negotiate in every situation.

I was flying from Mumbai to Chicago with British Airways. Unfortunately, my flight from Mumbai took off three hours late due to some engine issues and I missed my Chicago connection in London. The airline accommodated me on the next available flight, which was six hours later at 4.00 p.m. I alerted the airline staff that I had a checked-in bag and they should ensure that it is loaded into the 4.00 p.m. London–Chicago flight. 'Yes, of course, sir. Don't worry!' was the answer I got. When I reached Chicago, I was not sure if my bag had arrived. At the immigration counter, the polite officer asked me why I was looking hassled. I replied that I had missed my connection for no fault of mine and British Airways may not have loaded my bag. I had an early morning meeting and my shirts were in my checked-in luggage.

'Don't worry, sir. Ask the airline to buy you a fresh set of clothes. You are travelling business, right, they will pay you. Just ask!' was the advice from the immigration officer.

As suspected, my bag did not arrive. When I went to complain to the British Airways agent, I was told that since I missed my connection, the bag was still in London.

'Excuse me? I was on a flight that took off six hours later, but my bag was not loaded?' I did not say that with rancour but with a touch of humour.

The agent said, 'Well, Heathrow, you know.'

'But my clothes are in the checked-in bag. Now I need to buy new clothes. What can you do to help me, madam?'

'We will give you $20 for your trouble.'

'Twenty? But I travelled business class!'

The tone of the agent changed instantly. 'My apologies, sir. We will give you $100 and arrange for a limo to take you to your hotel. Your bag will be at the bell desk by noon tomorrow. Sorry for all the trouble.'

I would have missed out on the hundred dollars but for the immigration officer.

There is always a little bit to be made by asking the right questions. There is always some money on the table. The airline can upgrade you. The hotel can move you to a better room. They can always give you a late checkout. They can give you a complimentary drink. All you have to do is ask. Remember, in some cases, the other party could be trading something that is of very low value to them.

Negotiation is not something that we should be afraid of embracing. The tools and technique I have elucidated in this chapter can be applied to any situation you may encounter, from getting a better pay package to scoring a better price for your car or getting your customer to pay you a little bit more. Principles like reframing, thin slicing, enlarging the pie, overcoming biases, BATNA, ZOPA, using empathy and more can be applied any day, anywhere. Also remember SPANCO and probe > support > close are the magic mantras of selling. The terminology surrounding negotiation has changed over the decades, but the core principles are still relevant: don't react out of anger, put yourself in the other's shoes, attack the problem not the person and make it easy for the other side to say yes.

So, go forth and become a sales negotiation champion.

4
The Voice: Communication

All communication must lead to change.

—Aristotle

'Can you explain your product to us in a few minutes? We are hard-pressed for time.'

'We need you to complete your presentation in exactly thirty minutes. There are three other vendors waiting to meet us.'

'Your CV is impressive but can you tell us about your career journey in your own words? That will be a lot more interesting.'

'Can you send us a one-page note on your service offering?'

'Will you be able to make a presentation at our national sales conference to 500 of our top performers?'

A budding sales or business development executive is bound to have encountered several such challenges. However much you are prepared to take that call, there is always some twist in the tale. The time allotted gets cut down. Someone new is asked to meet you. Or, quite simply, the other party is not interested in what you are selling.

To be successful in marketing and sales, it is essential that we have finely honed communication skills—written and oral.

Where do we start?

What Is Communication?

In most companies, there is a wall between sales and marketing. Sales folk think that the marketing guys have a good time making ads and having fun; they don't understand the difficulties of selling a product in a hyper-competitive marketplace. Marketing folks feel that the sales guys are just price- and discount-focused and look for the next big offer or discount. Oftentimes, both are partly correct. Marketing is looking at the macro picture and brand health, while sales is focused on delivering the monthly numbers.

In my job at Boots as a member of the brand team, I had to make regular presentations to the sales managers. While there was a healthy respect for what each side did, there was an overhang of a feeling that they did not understand what we really do. Once, when preparing our annual presentation to the sales managers, we were told that we need to put ourselves in their shoes, simply because the **onus of the communication is on the communicator**. We cannot complain that the sales team does not understand the brand positioning or the brand communication—all the more important in a pharmaceutical sales situation, where the medical representative is really the medium. Some of us were not convinced that we (the brand team) should take 100 per cent responsibility for the communication. There is always a doubt if the other side is even willing to listen. What if they are set in their own ways? How can we take on the full responsibility? But eventually, we realised that communication was in our hands and unless we took full ownership, nothing could be achieved. Steven Covey talks about this in his book, *Seven Habits of Highly Effective People*: 'Being proactive is about taking responsibility for one's own life. Proactive people don't blame parents, circumstances, or conditions for their behaviour. Instead, they choose to focus on areas of life that lie within their circle of influence.' We have to figure out how to ensure communication takes place. While coaching senior executives, I often use this example and also point out that a good leader should be able to influence someone over whom they have no authority.

Nobel Laureate Richard Feynman used an interesting test to figure out if he had understood a concept—he would try and explain the concept to someone unfamiliar with it. If they understood what he had explained, Feynman would conclude that he too had understood the concept. The best way to learn a subject is to try and teach it to someone who is totally new to it. Similarly, unless you are able to explain it in simple terms so that the other person understands it, you are not clear about the concept yourself. Nowadays, you can say that if you can't create a Twitter-sized message about a concept, you have not understood it fully.

COMMUNICATION FLOW

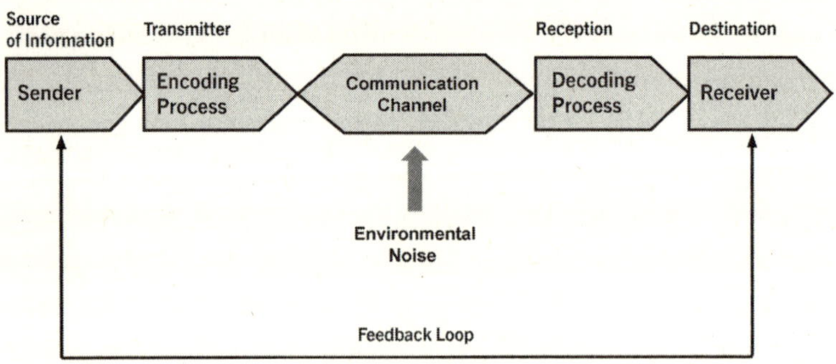

Communication flowchart

In communication theory, we are told that there is a sender and a receiver. The sender has a message they want to send to the receiver. The sender has to understand the message they want to send and, then encode it. Encoding could be a mail, a talk, a presentation, a film. This encoded message goes to the receiver. We cannot assume that the receiver will decode the message the same way that a sender encoded it; their interpretation will depend on their understanding of the topic, their pressures, etc. But if the message is decoded the way it was meant to be, then chances are that the receiver will be on the same page as the sender.

The case can be a brand manager sharing their annual plan with the sales managers from all over the country or a sales manager sharing ideas with his sales team. The same principle works again and again. While crafting any piece of communication, we need to ensure that we are on the same page as our intended receiver. If not, we will end up not getting the results want from the communication, whether you're at home, in the office, at a conference or in a board room.

Communication Framework

When planning any form of communication, be it one-on-one or one-to-many, you have to start with the definition of the target audience. Often, we don't spend enough time understanding the audience. I have been in many large forums where the speaker is making a presentation that is not curated for the listeners. As a result, two things happen. The audience thinks, 'We know all this, why is he repeating all that we know?' or 'What is he talking about? I don't understand a word of this.' The simplest homework is to get a clear understanding of the audience and change your presentation to suit it. Even if you have a profile of the target audience, it is important to study them as you deliver your talk to ensure that they are with you all the way.

The next step is to define the objective of the communication. In the case of the brand manager communicating to the sales managers, it is probably to get their support for the new brand campaign or promotion. Instead of just telling them about the promotion, it may be useful to ensure that you are engaged in a two-way communication.

While communicating, there are broadly three approaches: tell, sell, engage. The simplest and the least effective method is to tell: you announce the big promotion (say a 20 per cent discount for a limited period) that has been planned and how it will be a big success. The next (and somewhat better approach) is to sell: you explain the reasons why the promotion has been planned and how it will help the company. Sell works better than tell, always (unless it is an emergency and you are going to shout, 'FIRE!'). But even better than sell is engage: here, you engage the audience, you walk in their shoes and ensure that they are with you all the way. In the case of the discount offer, it may be good to get the sales team to see how it can help them open up new accounts, sell more to loyal buyers, etc., thereby helping them achieve their budgets.

You have understood your audience and your objective has been clearly delineated. Next, you want to figure out the big question: 'What's in it for me?' The audience should be clear that they will end up benefitting if they work with you on the promotion.

In marketing and sales, the modes of communication can be a face-to-face interaction or a presentation to a group of managers, to prospective customers or to an industry forum. Some of these will be simply verbal, while some of them may use audio-visual aids like a PowerPoint presentation or charts. When it comes to oral presentation, if you are in marketing or sales, you need to be able to speak. Gift of the gab, as we call it.

How can you develop this gift? Believe me, it can be developed. I remember when the competition 'Just a Minute' (JAM) was introduced at the IIT-M Mardi Gras festival. In this contest, the participant is given a topic and has to speak impromptu for one minute during which time they cannot repeat any words consecutively, stutter or pause for more than a second. While they are speaking, the other competitors watch and listen closely. If they spot a mistake, they can ring a bell, identify the fault and then take over the topic for the remainder of the minute, be it fifty-five seconds or five, for which they receive points. One of the first topics I remember was the line, 'She came in through the bathroom window' (a Beatles song); I remember Mahesh Krishnaswamy, several years my senior, speaking on it for one minute non-stop. We were in awe. Little did I know that someone who was watching this with me would go on to win the JAM contest a few years later. His magic recipe: practice, practice, practice. He went from being a speaker who would get tongue-tied after ten seconds to being able to speak on any topic for one minute without pausing or repeating the words more than once consecutively or stuttering.

If you want to be in marketing, it will do well for you to develop an ability to deliver an impromptu speech on any subject. Here are five for you to try. Your time starts now:

- How have consumers changed in the last ten years?
- Do corporate buyers only look at the price?
- What is the changing role of a retailer?
- How do you motivate your front-line sales team to do more?
- Is TV advertising dead?

Let us be clear, I don't think that, as a sales executive or a young brand manager, you will be asked to talk for one minute in front of the CMO about your new promotional offer or ad campaign. But it helps if you know how to do it, without hemming and hawing, fumbling for words and repeating the same ideas. One minute is a nice yardstick. In one minute, you can speak roughly 140–150 words. That may seem easy, but try practising in front of a mirror. Speak about anything for one minute. You will struggle the first few times, sure. But as you gain confidence, you will be able to speak for more than one minute with ease. As you master this, your admiration for great extempore orators will also increase.

What we discussed about oral presentation and speech is equally applicable to written communication. The same principles of sender – encode – message – decode – receiver are relevant here. Let us assume that you, as the sales training manager, are writing to the sales managers regarding a discussion on communication skills. This could be a one-page email. You need to apply the sender–receiver template to ensure that what you are writing will be decoded the same way you intended. In advertising, we have an approach for verifying if the Indian language translation is indeed accurate; one translator works on the English-to-Hindi translation; another translator is then given the Hindi translation and told to translate it back to English, as the case may be, to verify if the message is consistent (Google Translate can do the same job effortlessly).

What is true of an email is also true of everything you write. If you want to write a blog post, you need to adapt and apply all that you have learnt till now to it: Who is the target audience? What is your core message? Why should they read it? What is in it for them?

What is true of a 1,000-word article is also true of an 80,000-word book. I remember discussing this with Chandramouli Venkatesan (Mouli) whose book *Catalyst* was a runaway bestseller. Mid-2018, Mouli explained that when he was writing the book, he had a clear image of who that book was for: a person who was an executive, around thirty-three years old working a lower- to mid-level job in a large- or mid-sized company, trying to figure out how to manage their career. Mouli was also clear that he was not going to be preachy and would approach the 'engage/involve' model by pointing out incidents from his own career. Mouli had many books in his head and was planning on continuing his writing journey for many, many years. Unfortunately, he passed away on 6 October 2020 at the very young age of fifty-four after succumbing to pancreatic cancer.

Whatever your mode of communication, written or oral, long-form or short, big audience or small, the fundamentals of communication will always apply. Invest in understanding your target audience, make what you are saying relevant to them. The onus of the communication is with you—you need to figure out how your receiver is going to decode and interpret the message.

Now let us dig into specific types of communication. We start with one-on-one and then move on to other forms of communication.

One-on-One Communication

One-on-one communication comes in many shades in a marketing or sales job. To start with, you have to face an interview panel at your university. How well-prepared are you? Some schools arrange for mock interviews where senior students are requested to volunteer their time; this has got a huge fillip with the availability of platforms like Zoom and Microsoft Teams.

When going for an interview, you could apply all that we have learnt till now. When you speak, you are the sender of the message and the interviewer or the interview panel is the receiver. There may be three people on the panel. Are all of them receiving your message equally well?

In a business school, it is very difficult to know your interview panel. Which representative will come from which company may be a mystery, but past norms can give you a clear idea. There may be two people in the panel, one from human resources (HR) and one from marketing or sales. Most companies have a set system. Good business schools map these panels and provide students with an early warning; this HR head knows a lot about marketing, this one will quiz you on your people skills, etc.

Let us move from interview situation to a sales or business development situation. You have a meeting with an important prospect. How do you prepare for it? Again, you must apply the same rules. Find out who you are going to meet and their core skills. By using platforms like LinkedIn, you can get a good idea about your prospective customer. Once you have found out who the person is, you can then try and tailor your message. Some customers are all business and actively discourage small talk. Some others don't mind a bit of small talk before the sales pitch; speaking about a common alma mater is a good place to test the waters. If the response is lukewarm, quickly change the topic. As you start the meeting, you need to ascertain the time allocated. If the customer has provided one hour, be sure to keep at least fifteen minutes at the end for Q&As. One other tip is to befriend the secretary so that you get some extra time, if needed.

Appearances matter. As I have discussed in my book *All the World's a Stage,* there is something known as executive presence. How you appear, how you carry yourself into the room or how you walk influences how your message will be received. One simple rule of thumb is to dress one level better than the customer. If the customer is wearing a shirt, you should be in a formal shirt with maybe a jacket (a formal suit may be too much, just as a t-shirt could be too casual). In the start-up ecosystem, some of these rules don't apply. Find out if a t-shirt is the appropriate apparel so you don't show up in a three-piece suit when other high-ranking executives are in t-shirts and shorts.

Along with executive presence, your voice (often referred to as executive voice) matters. By voice, I don't just mean how you sound but also how you speak and the way you look. There are trainers who can work with you on your voice or, on YouTube, you can find enough gurus to help you along the way. Remember that speaking too quietly, too loudly, too fast or too slow are all issues. As Teddy Roosevelt put it, 'Speak softly and carry a big stick'—I suppose he meant that, as a world leader, you don't need to shout but you should know what your weapons are.

Let us assume you are in front of your prospect. You have spoken for a bit about your new product. What happens next? It is here that you have to learn something that, as an executive coach, I had to master, which is the art of active listening. In active listening, we engage with all our senses. Our body language indicates that we are absorbing what's being said. As Sheryl Sandburg says: lean in. Pay full attention. Look for the tone and manner of the communication. Don't interrupt for the sake of having the last word.

Of course, you do not have to agree with all that a prospect expresses. But you need to listen to all that they are saying and decide how to react only after they've concluded or you might interrupt an important thought that the prospect is attempting to put across.

As you continue with your discussion, don't forget to measure the progress you are making. If you are with a colleague, one of you should talk more while the other makes notes and measures progress.

Once, I remember meeting an important prospect and pitching our business to him. As the atmosphere in the room had mellowed and we were in a good zone, my colleague decided to talk about football. While the prospect was thrilled to bits that we had read about his interest in football, we only began discussing it after we had achieved a fair level of comfort. I am sure if we had started with football immediately, we would have ended up scoring a self-goal.

Let us say that you had a good meeting but while walking out, you stumble and almost fall down. Will this hurt your chances? It turns out that this may actually help you land the contract. Known as the pratfall effect, it refers to a phenomenon of a person who is seen as extremely competent becoming more likeable when they also commit a simple blunder. That simple blunder, the stumble, makes you appear more human. So if you spilled a little tea on your shirt or your file falls down or your pen leaked—the pratfall effect might save you.

One last tip about one-on-one selling situations that I used to give my team at Yellow Pages: if the prospect offers you tea at the beginning of the meeting, always say yes. Why? Simply because if the tea is delayed, you get extra time with the customer. Plus, saying no at the beginning can come across as rude. Let us flip the situation. The sale is done, the prospect is now a customer. They offer you a cup of tea. You should say no because in the time the tea arrives, the customer may ask more questions and end up regressing to a prospect again. As such, if the chemistry is good, you should simply thank them and quickly leave with the order in hand.

Communication to Groups

When you are in marketing or sales, you encounter a variety of one-to-many communication opportunities. You may be called upon to present to your internal team or to sales/marketing teams; we saw some shades of this at the beginning of this section. If you are in business development, presenting to prospects is your daily bread and butter. Then there are presentations you make to your customers about the solution you have tailored for them. Finally, there are talks and presentations you may be invited to.

Remember that in all these cases, some of the first principles still apply: sender–receiver paradigm; who/what/why/when.

Focusing on the wrong stuff while working on presentations.
Credit: Funny Business, *Shobha Prasad*

One-to-many communication could be to a group of ten customers or a hall full of over 200 potential customers. But the starting point is still the same. Who is the audience? You should have done your homework about them. If the information you have is incomplete, remember to read the room. All veteran presenters say that before they start the talk, they spend a few minutes reading the room. Musicians do this too, but they do it under the guise of testing the instruments. As a famous Carnatic singer once commented: 'If you think that before we start the concert, we spend a few minutes tuning the violin and the mridangam, you are sadly mistaken. The real tuning is done before the audience come in. We often do a second round to read the audience and give them time to settle down. We cannot start playing the electric guitar the moment we walk on to stage like a rock musician. We need the audience to get ready to soak in the music.' In a similar vein, before you start a presentation, you need to let the audience settle down and get ready to listen to your talk.

If you are going to present to a customer and have taken along some of your colleagues, it is a must that each of you has a specific role in the presentation. If only one person talks and the other three are nodding away, you make a poor impression. Ideally if it is a one-hour presentation, three people can take up twenty minutes each. Or even if one person is going to present, you need to create windows for the other three people in the room to speak. If you are the junior-most in the team, find out if you need to speak before the presentation starts. A top-class presenter might create what appears to be impromptu questions that are well-planned. For instance, when talking about customer connect, they may say: 'We believe in building our team from within. We have here Ritu, our youngest member who has spent three years with us. Ritu, can you tell the client the projects you have handled in the last two years?' Something simple like this can end up making a good impression.

Remember to read the room well and ensure that everyone has a role to play in the presentation.

Then comes the presentation aids. In my forty-five-year career, I have moved from handwritten charts and acetate sheets to Kodak carousel slides and PowerPoint presentations. AI-generated presentations are on their way. Some presenters prefer talking without any aids. If you are speaking at a large forum, it would be useful to find out if there is any norm you are expected to follow. For instance, TED and TEDx conferences have very specific guidelines about the duration of the talk, the kind of slides to be used, etc.

What should your PowerPoint presentation say? How many slides should you have? How complex should the slides be?

There is no rule of thumb, but you should budget for one minute per slide. A thirty-minute talk should have twenty-five to thirty-five slides.

What should be the text on the slides? In the past we used to follow the 4x5 rule. Each slide should have maximum four lines and each line should have maximum five words. But again, this is not a hard and fast rule. If the room is large and you have a huge audience, you may go for single-line slides. If you have a small audience, you may go for complex slides. I have noticed that management consultants tend to have slides that are very complicated. Each slide could take five minutes for a deep dive.

Graphics on slides are great as long as they don't distract. Remember that you want to achieve something specific with your talk, and every element should help you in your journey. Great graphics may make an impact, but if they don't serve your primary purpose, it is best to go with simple ones.

How often have you been in a talk or a presentation where the speaker is droning on and on, and you wished they would stop? It is important for the speaker to keep reading the audience. If the audience is showing signs of discomfort, stop and throw out a question or speed up to a different topic. Remember: *the onus of the communication is on the communicator*. You cannot say that the audience was not receptive that day. It is your job to make them respond to your talk. If required, swich gears to take questions midway or let someone else in the team take over.

I remember a talk by a direct marketing guru. We had invited him to do a one-hour seminar for select customers and prospects. As his presentation progressed, I realised that he was jumping around the topics. Fortunately, we had built him up as a 'guru' and an author of a much-respected book, so the audience was patient. After he was done, I had to ask him how he thought the seminar went. He, being a veteran, confessed he performed below par, and the problem had been that the PowerPoint presentation he had been using was not the right version. He regretted not having stopped after he realised the faux pas to reset. The lesson to me was that when in doubt, stop. If required, rewind and restart.

At the end of your presentation, your audience should not say 'What a boring talk!' or 'A fun discussion, but what were they trying to say?' Both those outcomes are suboptimal.

If it went well, the audience should say, 'We learnt so much from that talk. It ended too soon, when can we hear her again?'

There is this simple three-question feedback a friend once told me to ask the audience:

- What was one thing I said that you already knew?
- What in the talk was something new to you?
- What in the talk was unexpected—a wow moment?

As you complete your talk in a forum, you should expect questions. If you don't get any questions, you have had one of two problems. Either the presentation was so boring that the audience could not be bothered to ask you any questions, or it was so complex that no one understood anything. Sometimes, in order to get a Q&A going, some of the better organisers seed some questions beforehand, which helps gets the audience in the mood of asking questions.

Irrespective of the audience size, there is only one mantra to success: prepare, prepare, prepare. Before your presentation, you have to know your material really well. You should know your slides like the back of your hand. You should know the order of the slides and the link sentences between them. If the presentation has three chapters, you need to know when the chapter breaks come and what you should do at those moments.

Often, when you are in the audience and you hear a great speaker, you are spellbound. You wonder how they are making such a talk almost extempore. Remember, the talk is never extempore. There must have been endless hours of practice.

As a young brand manager, I have had to go through endless presentations in front of my boss before every regional managers' meeting. Often, each of us had to go through these practice sessions several times till we got everything right. And even after that happened, we had to do one more round. In advertising too, I have had the job of sitting through many rounds of presentations till all of us were convinced that we had it all down pat. Everyone had to know every single slide and could step in for another speaker if required. And there was a predetermined place for each speaker. A good presentation is nothing short of a well-conducted orchestra or theatre. As someone once told me when I asked them what is the difference between an amateur and a professional: 'An amateur practises till they get it right. A professional practises till they cannot get it wrong.'

If you want to be good at one-to-many communication, you need to practise till you cannot get it wrong.

> 'I notice that you use plain, simple language, short words and brief sentences. That is the way. The best way. Stick with it.'
>
> —*Mark Twain in a letter to a friend*

Written Communication

In marketing, and in organisations, a lot of communication is done through the written mode. And more than any other department in a company, the marketing group probably has to do more written communication. The digital revolution has just increased the volume, variety and velocity of communication. To get some perspective, in the 1970s and 1980s, employees who worked in far-flung areas had very limited methods of communicating with their superiors. The faithful landline was used sparingly since it was expensive. All sales representatives and territory managers had to write daily reports, and often they were also encouraged to write a monthly report about their respective territory. As a young brand manager, I used to go through the more than 100 reports that used to come to the marketing department from the field managers. These contained a lot of useful information about market trends, competitor activities and more.

Cut to 2025. All sales executives are on 24x7, communicating with their bosses and customers. Today, there are field apps that a sales executive can access and get real-time support during a sales call.

One thing has not changed: the ability to communicate via the written word. In the past, it used to be pen and paper. Then it became the computer and email. Now it is the smartphone and app-based communication. In all these mediums, if you don't know how to string a few sentences together, you are not going to be able to put your message across.

We only spoke of sales executives and company communication. The same is true when you deal with customers. Today, customers are accessible via digital media and ready to engage with business development teams.

There are, however, several pitfalls along the way.

For instance, just because you are communicating with your boss or customer by WhatsApp, should you adopt a casual approach and pepper your message with emojis and abbreviations like 'ttyl'? Or will the Queen's English sound too pompous when used in a WhatsApp message? What is the right level of formality in communication? If you are on friendly terms with your customer or boss, you can take a casual approach. But if you are not sure, it is better to stick close to a formal mode of communication.

Unfortunately, a lot of written business communication in India is in English. And we are going to be seeing more and more young men and women entering the corporate world with a poor knowledge of English, written and spoken. What should be done?

Even in leading business schools like IIM Ahmedabad, one of the most memorable courses is on communication. Called

'Written Analysis and Communication', or WAC, it is a course that makes a lasting impact on all the business school graduates. It coaches first-year MBA students on the importance of business communication, oral and written. Through exercises and case studies, participants are made to understand the key tenets of communication that we have been discussing in this chapter. In addition, participants are sensitised to the seven Cs of communication: completeness, conciseness, consideration, clarity, concreteness, courtesy and correctness. Completeness elicits the desired response. Being concise in communication saves time (we will look at the other side of conciseness in a bit). Consideration is the art of understanding human behaviour. Clarity makes communication clear with no scope for ambiguity (onus of the communication is on the communicator). Concreteness, proof, reinforces confidence. Courtesy reinforces mutual respect. Correct use of grammar and vocabulary builds confidence.

Many of us may not have had the benefit of a top-grade MBA education, but that should not deter anyone. There are several written communication workshops that you can attend to hone in your skills. Recently, I attended a writing workshop conducted online by Amit Verma (who also has a highly rated long-form podcast called 'The Seen and The Unseen' on which I was his 199th guest). It is never too late to improve yourself.

To start with, you need to get a fix on where you stand currently. How comfortable are you when you are asked to write a memo or a report? Do you have a process that you follow when you have to write a report? Are you more familiar with a pen or a keyboard?

In written communication, your vocabulary matters. This does not mean you have to use complex words (leave that to Shashi Tharoor). Remember, using big words does not make you an intellectual. There are many online tools for you to use to measure the quality and complexity of your writing. One test I have found useful is the Gunning Fog Index. On this website you can cut and paste what you have written and the tool will tell you how complex, vocabulary-wise is your writing. If you copy paste what you have written into the Gunning Fog Index website, you will know how many years of schooling a person should have to go through in order to understand what you are trying to write. Even if your audience is highly educated, experts tell us that a score of 8 or 9 is ideal. For example, I put the above two paragraphs through the Gunning Fog Index and got a score of 8.2; that is, in order to understand what I have written, the reader should have had eight years of formal school education. When I conduct communication workshops for corporates, I ask the participants to post what they had recently written into the Gunning Fog Index website; some of them score an 8 and there are always some who score over 14! That is not such a good thing.

Don't get me wrong. I am not against jargon or abbreviations. When writing to a customer who knows the meaning of 'stupendous', you can use that word. But it may be safer to go with something simpler like 'excellent' or 'great'. Similarly, when writing to someone who knows the subject, you may get away with a sentence such as 'Our GRP levels are below threshold'; but if that person is not as clued in to marketing, then something on the lines of 'our advertising inputs are probably below a level that can make an impact on consumers' works better. The second sentence is a little long, but someone who does not know technical jargon will also be able understand what you are trying to say.

How can you improve your writing skills? There are some simple hacks. First, you might need to read a lot more than you are doing now. If you are reading for twenty minutes a day (and I don't mean WhatsApp forwards), increase that to thirty minutes. Try reading articles and op-ed pieces in newspapers. There are several excellent writers such as Shekhar Gupta, Vir Sanghvi, Santosh

Desai who write in popular newspapers. Read their columns regularly.

The next important step is to start writing. Even if you have not been invited to write a column in *The Economic Times* or *The Hindu*, you can write a short piece of 700 words and post it on your LinkedIn page. If you can write an article every few weeks, you will discover that it grows on you.

Coming to business communication, be it an email or a report, apply the cardinal rules of communication. Who is the target audience? What do you want them to learn from your communication? Why should they react? When should they receive your message?

I have a few other simple tips to ensure that you don't make some of the mistakes I have made.

When you get a message that is not so pleasant, say, a customer rejecting your offer, you might be tempted to respond immediately. Don't. You can write a reply but save it to drafts. Go back to the draft after twenty-four hours. Your mood may have changed and you might find that you wish to change the reply as well.

In the introductory training given to young executives, I always insist that before sending a mail to a client, one should read it twice. Remember, it can be forwarded to others and cause untold damage. I even give the example of a young enthusiastic executive who once wrote in the email to a client '... this is so clear that only a single-digit IQ person will not understand what I am trying to say ...' Obviously, this got the young executive into some trouble. This little incident was remembered for many years as the 'Single-Digit IQ Faux Pas'!

Beware of the traps of forwarding emails super-fast. People often make the mistake of forwarding an email without checking and clearing the trail mail.

Do not equate WhatsApp to casual communication. All communication, irrespective of the medium, has to be seen in the same light. While the statement 'the medium is the message' is true, you cannot take chances if you don't know your recipient well.

There is a famous quote attributed to the French mathematician and philosopher Blaise Pascal. He is reported to have said in a longish letter: 'I have made this longer than usual because I have not had time to make it shorter.'

Those are profound words. A longer message does not necessarily mean it is a better piece of communication. You can communicate better if you spend time in crafting your message to the right level of brevity. Some global companies even have a one-page rule: managers are trained to write a succinct one-page memo on their proposal. Jeff Bezos is reported to have banned PowerPoint presentations; he prefers his team members to read a five-page memo silently for thirty minutes and then discuss the issues. I feel presentations are important but, of course, sitting through a long presentation when you are pressed for time can be a recipe for disaster.

Integrated Marketing Communications

We are now nearing our final destination. What distinguishes marketing folks from all others in an organisation? They are the agents who orchestrate the company's communication. We took one look at this in the chapter on brand building. But it is now time to dive a little deeper.

To start, you may wonder what we mean by integrated marketing communication. Isn't it the same as advertising? Well, not really. What was once called advertising is now part of a larger range of services we refer to as integrated marketing communication, or IMC.

What we call advertising has been in existence for centuries. Merchants used to paint their names on boards and hang them outside their premises. Some merchants sent out town criers to call out their offerings. When printing took off, they published leaflets and distributed them in town squares. Advertisements began appearing in newspapers. Ad agencies emerged to help manufacturers and merchants craft their messaging. Initially, ad agencies acted as agents of newspapers; they earned a commission for each ad they placed in a newspaper. Over time, they have become more and more client-focused and the old agency commission model of payment has diminished in importance.

Over many decades, advertising diversified as media expanded. As competition increased, brands had to think of new ways of engaging with consumers. What we today call 'experiential marketing' started gaining ground. In the early days, this referred to product launches held in hotels where you invited your dealers and engaged with them on the new product. Slowly, companies realised that inviting important customers to product launches is key. Companies in the IT sector made this into a regular annual event. Steve Jobs made the annual events into product launch extravaganzas. Dhirubhai Ambani made his annual general meeting of shareholders into a forum for making big announcements. Mukesh Ambani has followed that tradition.

Digital media started growing in importance in the 2010s. Companies that used to have brochures started having websites. And as technology changed, these websites became interactive, packed with useful information and videos.

The growth of social media offered brands yet another way of engaging with consumers. Brands started becoming active on all social media platforms, often using hundreds of influencers.

Today if you were to analyse the data, every brand is active in more than half a dozen domains. If it is a consumer product like a soap, then you will be advertising on television, window displays at stores, radio, print, website and social media. If you are a high-end software, then you may be on technical journals/websites, your own website, IT shows/exhibitions, consumer meets, information videos, etc.

As such, what was once advertising has now become more multi-faceted. The challenge is to ensure that all these various forms of communication do not end up confusing the consumer. This resulted in the idea of creating one unifying subject to study: integrated marketing communications.

IMC is the art and science of understanding and using various marketing communication platforms in a way that they all add to the overall brand message. The challenge is to ensure that the various platforms do not pull in different directions and cause confusion in the market. You can't be lazy about communication too; just translating the key message for each medium is not enough. You may want to recraft the message entirely to suit the nuances of the medium. As Marshall McLuhan observed many decades ago, the medium is the message—his words still ring true as we are surrounded by multiple media options to use. Today, experts talk of 'high attention media' and 'low attention media'; television and print can be seen as high attention while Instagram is low attention. Each medium works differently based on our learning and memory skills.

If a company had one ad agency in the 1960s, today they probably deal with half a dozen agencies: ad, media, digital, PR, event agencies and more. How to ensure that all of them communicate the same message? How to get them to act in a synergistic manner?

We should start with what is known as the six Ms of IMC: market, mission, message, media, money and measurement.

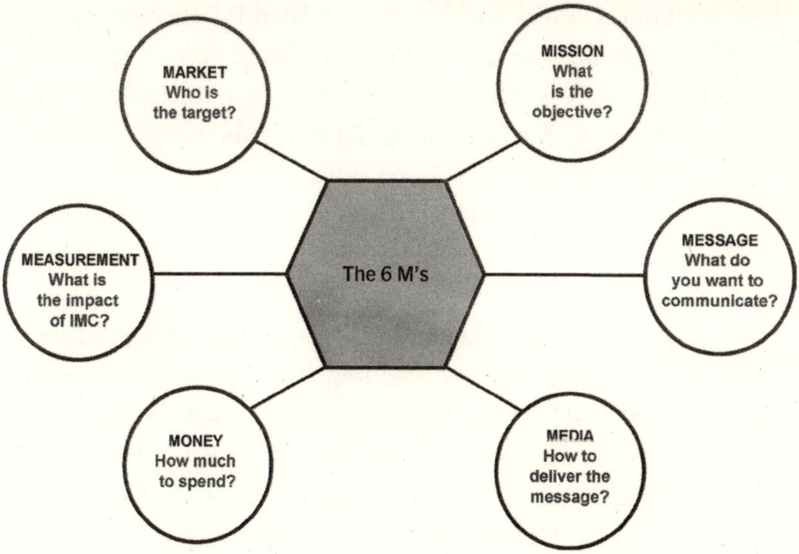

The six M's of integrated marketing communication

The first task of IMC is to figure out the **market** you want to attract—who is the target of the message. Before embarking on any IMC activity, it is necessary to get a clear definition of the target market. The more sharply defined it is, the better your IMC efforts will be. If you are launching a new premium healthy RTC range of food products, who will you go after? All women or working women who have less time? Or affluent working couples who have the money, not time, but are concerned about health? As you can see, the better the target definition, the better your next 5Ms will be.

Now we have the market defined. We then define what is going to be our **mission**. Is it to get 30 per cent of all affluent families to try the new product or to get 20 per cent to become regular users? What is the mission of the IMC programme?

The next and probably most important step is to capture the right **message**. A lot of time is spent crafting the message or the core of the communication since the message's strategy will emerge from product- and consumer-related information. What is different about your offer? How is it different from all the other products available in the market? Shouting from the rooftop may not do the trick. You need to understand whether your target consumer will be interested in that story.

Once the message is crafted, you then get into planning **media**. Where will this message appear? In newspapers? In digital media? The message may work better in one medium and not so well in another. Your brand may have a stronger action focus, so you may want to depict activities (like Red Bull) that will excite your consumer. Planning media does not just mean number-crunching. Digital media is used by brands for what is known as performance marketing; mass media is used for brand marketing. Sometimes these two don't talk to each other, that is a challenge.

Media planning cannot be done without having a fix on the **money** that we have available to spend. The estimation of IMC money will come from your overall business strategy. I am asked by companies, 'How much should we spend on IMC?' The answer varies depending on where you are. If you are a mature brand in a mature category, say detergent powder, then your IMC spends may be in the region of 10 per cent of your sales revenue. If you are a category that is growing fast in India, like cosmetics, then your IMC spends may be higher than 15 per cent. But if you are a new brand that has great growth ambitions and a large budget, then your IMC budget may even be bigger than your sales revenue. Look at the way some start-ups burn cash; their losses are higher than their revenue. Who is funding them and why? Their investors are probably hoping that after the initial few years, the consumer acquisition cost (CAC) will taper off and the company will enter a positive cash-flow situation. But not all companies manage to make that transition.

The final M is **measurement**. What are you getting for all the money you are spending? Traditional marketing was focused on measuring sales, market shares and share of voice. What should you spend if want to increase your market share by 1 per cent; assuming you have a 10 per cent of the category and your share of voice or share of spend is 11 per cent (that is, you are spending 11 per cent of what the category spends on IMC), how do you increase your market share by increasing your ad spends? Models have shown that, given all things being constant, you can increase your market share to 12 per cent if you also increase your share of spends to 16 per cent. The problem is that this is expensive, and you may not achieve this goal without entering the loss-making zone. In performance marketing done through digital advertising, you are constantly measuring every incremental rupee you spend. What is the cost of getting a click? A lead? An order? You have all the data to tell you what works best for your brand. Today, measurement has become the true mantra for companies.

While we have six Ms of IMC in terms of communication, the most important one is the message. What should the message be? How to ensure that it will work?

To help your agency partner develop the right message, it is imperative that you provide them with a brief. Most good briefs contain several specific elements:

1. Why are we communicating? What is the problem we are solving?
2. What do we expect communication to do? How do we measure its success?
3. Whose behaviour are we trying to affect? What insights do we have about them? What is the insight about the consumer?
4. What is the competitive opportunity? Who will lose if we win?
5. What is the key takeaway of our message?
6. Why is this true? What is the reason to believe?

7. How do we say it? What will be our tone and manner, our brand hallmarks, our executional guidelines?
8. What are some guidelines on dos and don'ts?
9. What are some thought starters (initial ideas from brand team)?

Companies use various tests to ensure that they have the right message. One simple acronym is the RUB test—relevant, unique, believable. Is the message relevant to your target market; will they find it useful, interesting? Being relevant is not enough, since there are many brands that are relevant. So you have to be unique, different from all the others. Here, companies can hit a wall if their products are similar in nature. Can you dig deeper to find something that is different about your brand? If you can say something that no one else is saying, it is unique to you. Finally, what you communicate needs to be believable. You have to ensure that what you say is not dismissed by your customers as hot air. If your message is relevant, unique and believable, you improve your chance of success.

Yet another way of evaluating your message is the three-filter test—brand filter, communication filter, campaign filter. If you are evaluating an ad, the first question you need to ask is, 'Is the ad true to what our brand offers?' This is the brand filter. The ad has to reflect the brand's promise. The next question is, 'Is the ad engaging to a consumer who is highly distracted?' This is the communication filter. You may have an ad that is on brand promise but is very boring. Consumers will not remember the ad or the brand. The last filter is 'Can this idea be extended?' In the era of IMC, every idea has to have legs to travel into other media, and over many years. This is the campaign filter. If your communication passes the three-filter test, you have a winner in your hands.

Let us not forget that IMC ten years ago is no longer the same. There was a time when clients briefed agencies and agencies returned with their communication ideas after a few weeks. The ideas that were approved became campaigns that ran for a year or much longer. This cycle time has dramatically come down in the 2020s. Today, a campaign that runs on TV may be briefed, created and released in just a few weeks. In my experience, I have only once created a campaign and got it on air in less than four weeks (read about it in the chapter 'Decisions Made Rapidly' in my book *Sponge: Leadership Lessons I Learnt from My Clients*). Nowadays, on social media, it is likely that a brand puts out thirty messages, maybe even sixty messages a month in mixed media formats. How can you ensure that all sixty messages are aligned to what the brand is all about? How to ensure that you don't end up with a fiasco?

Fortunately, most of the messages do not stick around for a long time, so small errors can be missed by the public. But there are cases where a brand posts a message on Instagram that catches fire.

This is where IMC again comes to your rescue. If you have a good IMC team, you should be monitoring digital and social media round the clock so you can spot the problem before it becomes a full-blown crisis. Big brands have large social media listening stations where a team monitors the internet chatter around the brand and its competitors. If you are a small entrepreneur, you also should be concerned about the reviews posted by people on platforms. You need to monitor them on a regular basis and offer to reach out if there are issues that have been pointed out.

No doubt everything we know about IMC will change over the following decade. What will be next? Will AR/VR take over? Will AI manipulate us into buying things we don't really need? Imagine tapping your smartphone to see a virtual image of the new shoe you want to buy. Or walking into a department store and the camera recognises you as a regular customer, flashes a welcome message and tells you about the arrival of a new shoe. Today, we pay using our mobile phones. A day will be upon us where we can pay by just looking at a camera. People have already begun paying for their coffee by tapping their smartwatch against the card reader machine.

Ten years ago, making a video message was a complex process. Apps like TikTok have made this so easy that there is a virtual video content tsunami. All this has already begun to affect brand communication.

The question remains, what should a brand do? Should every brand become a so-called content factory? For example, should a shampoo brand invest in making hundreds of videos about hair care or engage with influencers to create videos? Whatever you focus on should produce the best results—that will help you maximise your return on marketing investments.

There are two big pitfalls that I have seen affecting brands. One is to see India as a single market. In reality, India is a federation of many markets. Several brands have been able to achieve success by not going all-India, but into regional market after market. The other big pitfall is to try and tick all the boxes offered by IMC, that is, doing a little bit of many things but not achieving genuine impact on any of the platforms used.

Prayer may be the last key for brand success. Credit: Funny Business, *Shoba Prasad*

A few years ago, I remember speaking to a seasoned CMO to know how she allocated her marketing money in this digital era. She candidly admitted that she adopted the S&P method: spray-and-pray method. Obviously, she was joking. What she probably did was allocate money across, say, twenty initiatives and hope two or three of them worked. When she saw something working, she would double down and increase allocation to that platform.

I suppose S&P may give way to more sophisticated methods. As platforms and algorithms change, complexities may continue to increase—and brand IMC champions will have to run very hard to stay in the same place.

> 'If you invest in long-term partnerships across the board, whether it is a media agency, creative agency, business agency, any vendor ... and if you make them understand your brand, they can also take the brand far, far ahead with you.'
>
> —*Vivek Sharma, CMO, Pidilite Industries*

Complete Communications

If you are in marketing, you need to fine-tune your communication competencies. Your communication skills will be put to test the day you walk into the interview room. You may be asked to talk about your life journey in one minute. Remember the exercise I suggested: stand in front of your bathroom mirror and speak for just a minute (JAM) non-stop. A minute may seem a short amount of time but you will soon discover that you are searching for words at the forty-second mark. Practise some of these topics: Why do you want to be in sales? What sets you apart from your batchmates? What is one thing you can do well? What is the one failure that you cannot forget and what did you learn from it? My book *Spring: Bouncing Back from Rejection* will give you some fodder.

If you clear the interview process, chances are you will be made to work in frontline sales. This will mean speaking with customers and prospects; you may meet ten to forty customers a day depending on your industry. This will be an opportunity to improve your communication skills—you will be able to practise how to tailor your message to suit every customer by understanding where they are coming from. The principles we studied will all be relevant irrespective of where you are working, Mumbai or Nanded.

Often when working in field sales, you lose the ability to write well. That is quite understandable, since you are on the road all the time. Where is the time to sit and write? But if you want to build your career in marketing, you have to find the time to read and write. I remember being sent on a field visit when I joined my first job in advertising. My boss felt that instead of working in an air-conditioned office, I (along with the others who had joined as management trainees) should spend time working in the market. I was told to head to Rajasthan to work with the sales representative of one of our clients. This was at the height of summer. Over one month, I worked with Mr Jethani, covering more than fifteen small towns of Rajasthan. For the sake of discipline, I would write a one-page report every day on what I had learnt, send it back to the head office and keep a carbon copy of the report for my records. When I got back to Mumbai, my superiors complimented me on having built this habit, especially the observations I had made about each small town. Maybe this is what got me a posting in Mumbai, while the other two who had joined with me were sent to Chennai and Kolkata. Moral of the story: don't underestimate the power of written communication.

Most good companies move trainees from sales to marketing and then back to sales. They may also move you to other departments like operations, HR, etc. Folks who have cut their teeth in marketing are expected to be better communicators—irrespective of the department you are assigned to, you will find that your communication skills will come to your aid. I know of several youngsters who started their career by working in the office of an executive director of a company and rising rapidly thanks to their impeccable communication skills.

We saw the importance of one-on-one oral communication, one-to-many oral communication, written communication and IMC. While each of them sounds different, the fundamentals remain the same: the onus of the communication is on the communicator. You cannot say that, 'I wrote a clear report but the customer did not understand what was said!' To be an effective communicator, you need to follow the steps outlined: who is the target audience; what do you want to achieve with your communication; why should they listen to you; what is the desired reaction from them; how will you measure the outcome.

Irrespective of the situation, from a one-minute opportunity to speak with the CEO to an hour-long presentation to the board, the fundamentals don't change. Poor communicators get carried away with their own train of thought. Good communicators remain focused on the target audience. They know that the only purpose of communication is to move the recipient from Point A to Point B. Be aware of the purpose of your communication and the impact it is having. As George Bernard Shaw put it, 'The single biggest problem in communication is the illusion that it has taken place.'

Summing Up and Planning Ahead

This book would have given you a good idea about what I think are four crucial skills to be successful in marketing: understanding consumers, brand building, selling and negotiation and communication. But to be successful in marketing, is that all you need to know? Not really. Let's pull back and look at the bigger picture.

What can make you successful in marketing? A good MBA degree from one of the top business schools? A starting job in a dream company? A mentor who helps you reach your goal quicker than anyone else?

> 'Marketing is common sense business that is done in sunshine. You can't perfect it in a lab. You can't put it in an Excel spreadsheet. You have to work with people.'
>
> —*Shubhranshu Singh, VP, Marketing, Domestic & IB, CVBU, Tata Motors*

Hard Skills (Core Skills) and Soft Skills (Impact Skills)

In order to succeed in any job, you need to have the critical hard skills required to fulfil your key role in an organisation. For instance, if you are a chef, you need to know how to cook, what ingredients to use and what process to follow. These are hard skills or core skills. But in addition to that, you need to have several critical soft skills to be able to create the impact that will take you forward. Again, taking the same example, to be a successful chef, you'd need to have the soft skills of team work, creativity, communication, adaptability, customer engagement, etc. In essence, you will need a combination of soft and hard skills. Obviously in order to succeed in marketing as well, you need several hard and soft skills. You cannot ignore one for the sake of the other.

Core Skills in Marketing

By now you would have grasped that you need to have several core skills that are essential to enter the marketing department. This book has covered four of the most essential hard skills necessary for that. However, to be successful in marketing, you need many more core skills. Covering all those will make this book a bulky read, but let me touch upon a few more core skills.

One of the important skills is **the go-to-market (GTM) skill**. It is not just enough to have a well-crafted brand and a good ad campaign. How are you going to reach the end user? In the past, most FMCG or consumer product brands had a clear route to market: set up a sales force and start supplying the product to the general trade. But in the last ten years, many more options have emerged. Several start-ups have avoided the expensive process of setting up a full-fledged sales team and have instead gone directly to consumers through e-commerce platforms. In India, unlike in many other parts of developed world, general trade or the mom-and-pop shops are continuing to thrive. At the same time, modern or organised trade is becoming a force to reckon with. The old system of wholesalers is under some pressure. In essence, for a consumer product, the GTM strategy can involve several of these channels. In the case of other product categories, there are similar scenarios playing out. Electronic goods have seen an extraordinary boom in sales through e-commerce platforms. Some direct-to-consumer (D2C) cosmetic brands have managed to achieve great success through social media marketing and influencer-led campaigns.

When it comes to B2B products, GTM may involve finding the prospects who have the most potential to accept the offering and launch it to the larger audience. Be it B2B or B2C, GTM also involves building a sales team to take your product or service to the market. How big should the team be, what should be the competencies of the team, what kind of training should be imparted to them? In my conversation with CMOs, it was clear that most of them had spent time in sales and cherished the learning they gained from it. Most of them consider GTM an essential skill that separates those who can plan and those who can plan and implement. Setting up a sales team and managing and motivating it is an essential core skill.

Digital marketing has emerged as an essential skill irrespective of the kind of product or service being marketed. In essence, it is the way a company uses digital methods to communicate, engage and sell its products and services to its customers. If we take an FMCG product, it can mean selling the product on platforms like Amazon or from the company's own website. It can mean advertising and sharing information about the features of the product on digital channels such as YouTube or Instagram. Companies can also engage with consumers through their social media handles. Today, a disgruntled consumer can share their grievances on social media and cause untold damage to a brand. The good thing about this is that a company can turn the situation around with some strategic PR. Monitoring digital media is a vital part of marketing communication. Some industries are a little behind in adopting digital marketing, but they're catching up. Even in B2B businesses, some companies have been able to leverage the power of digital tools to solicit leads, share learnings through blog posts and videos and almost create an alternate mode of selling. During the COVID-19 pandemic, many sectors that were dependent on physical contact moved to digital platforms. For instance, pharmaceutical brands have adopted multiple digital tools to get their message across to healthcare professionals, using tools like Zoom and MS Teams to host webinars. Post-pandemic, most have returned to face-to-face detailing of brands, but Zoom webinars have continued to flourish. There are many books and online courses on digital marketing, but it is worth remembering that the terrain is changing rapidly. A book or a course created in 2015 may no longer be relevant in 2025.

With the data deluge, marketing has to handle the big data challenge. What is big data? From the days when we used to analyse sales- and marketing-related data on a once-a-month basis, today we have a constant volume of a variety of data flowing in 24/7. Given this data deluge, to be successful in marketing, you need to understand the contours of **data analytics**—what data to capture, what to analyse and how frequently the analysis should be done. Data is just the raw material. Analysis converts it into useful information. Deeper study of this information leads to actionable insights. Why is our website traffic increasing? Why are orders dropping? What is the buzz around the brand? Why is the competitor getting so many positive mentions on social media? Add to this the usual data about sales, market shares, share of voice in media, and you can well imagine the amount of data that can be analysed. The tragedy is that many marketing executives get excited about setting up data analytics teams that can crunch through reams of data—but having a team just to crunch data is not enough, you need to have the competencies to derive actionable information from that. With the availability of powerful computers and data analysis tools, data analytics is an important skill in all areas of a company, B2B/B2C and policymaking.

To be successful in marketing, you need to understand how to stretch your marketing budgets and **optimise the return on marketing investments** or **ROMI**. Managing ROMI is a core skill, I have noticed, that most successful marketing executives hold. It is imperative that managers try to understand the various accounting and financial implications of all their decisions. Will a change in packaging result in costs shooting up? Will we be able to amortise the cost of an expensive marketing project over two years? If we increase our marketing spends by another 10 per cent, what will be the impact on sales revenue? Will a price increase result in a drop in volumes—and how will this impact the bottom line? Managing marketing finances will give you a crucial edge in an industry that is numbers-oriented.

CMOs need to be able to think in terms of operations and strategy simultaneously. **Strategic marketing** is a core skill that looks beyond the immediate impact and focuses on the long-term implications of marketing actions. A good CMO should be able to both zoom in and zoom out—look at a problem from a bird's eye view and also from the ground level. For example, a sales promotion may deliver short-term sales, but will it affect long-term brand equity? One of the most quoted examples of an inability to zoom out is the case of the American railroad industry—how they defined their business as a railroad sector and not as 'transportation', leading to huge erosion in business and profitability as they did not see road transport as competition. A good CMO should be able to look at the big picture, the adjacencies, the substitutes, the complementary products and services to ensure the long-term success of a company.

> 'In the formative years of your career, you must try and make as many mistakes as you can and get as much learning as you can. Because that's when the organisation will actually be the most willing and receptable to some of the mistakes you would make.'
>
> *—Anshul Khanna, Senior Director of Marketing, Foods, Pepsico India*

Soft Skills or Impact Skills for Marketing

Hard skills alone cannot ensure your success in marketing. You need the help of soft skills to create impact in the organisation. No matter which department you may be working in, you will need a set of soft skills, and these may be common across all functions in a company and will help you create the right impression that will take you forward. These skills help you interact effectively with others around you and ensure that you are able to get things done.

In my conversations with twenty-nine CMOs, it came through that they were all masters of soft skills. All of them could communicate well, build a team and manage team morale, had great work ethic and were able to apply creativity and critical thinking to their job. From my conversations with them, I have identified a few key skills. Let us look at them one by one.

Working with a team is an important soft skill. In marketing, you get to deal with a number of departments inside the company, such as product development, manufacturing, finance, supply chains, etc. Unless you can build team spirit with all of them, you will not be able to deliver the goods. Even outside the company, it's usually the marketing department that has the greatest number of external partners: distributors, retailers, ad agencies, packaging suppliers, product development partners, market research, digital and PR agencies, merchandising partners, event, design and media agencies, media owners/sellers, etc. A good CMO can build a strong relationship with many of them, moving from a simple vendor or a buyer-seller relationship to one of partnership. In my career in advertising, I have met so many great CMOs who treated their agencies not as just suppliers of creative but as true mind partners (I have captured some of those lessons in my book *Sponge: Leadership Lessons from My Clients*).

To be effective in marketing, you have to able to **think outside the box**. It could be a new packaging option, a pricing plan, an ad campaign or a sales promotion. No other department offers so many opportunities for you to be creative. As such, creative thinking is a very important soft skill. What do we mean by creative thinking? It is the ability to think differently and do things that your competitor has not. There are specific ways to generate ideas. One way is brainstorming—a meeting where a team is allowed to present all their ideas, good, bad and ugly ones, with no criticism. The ideas are then sorted for their actionability. Better CMOs stimulate their teams to be creative with the understanding that if an idea fails, it will not affect the career of the colleague. When it comes to ad agency partners, the better CMOs I have dealt with are willing to let the agency suggest ideas that may be outside the brief and are willing to take calculated risks with their marketing budgets. In fact, when encouraged, an agency tends to present better and better ideas. Creativity is not just restricted to advertising; consumer research, events, merchandising and sales promotions can all be done creatively. All told, marketing offers many avenues to be creative. The better CMOs understand this and encourage their teams and their outside partners to try out innovative concepts and campaigns.

What happens when you hit a roadblock, when your brand sales declines or brand health scores fall steeply? You can panic and pull all the levers or you can **apply critical thinking/problem-solving skills**. By doing so, you will start asking questions about all the assumptions that you may have made. For example, Toyota has popularised the five-why technique to unravel the issues behind a problem. Why have sales declined? The answer to this may be 'seasonality'. Why is seasonality important for our brand? And so on. Critical thinking is a way of exiting the box of assumptions you may have climbed into while developing your marketing plan. Plus, CMOs need to apply critical thinking not just when things go south but also when things are going well. For instance, if we don't understand why our brand is exceeding the budget, we may end up assuming that the brand has gained instant strength, while the real issue may be the shortage of a key competitor's product.

Do things happen as planned, always? What other soft skill is needed to ensure that things go the way you want? A good CMO knows that without a great degree of **organisational skills and planning skills**, a marketing plan will never get off the ground. To ensure that a plan gets delivered requires a great deal of organisational intelligence. To start with, you need to understand the moving parts and how they all come together (or in a bad case, come apart).

Successful CMOs know that the difference between a good marketing campaign and a great marketing campaign could be timing. A campaign that is executed in time can produce great results. Hence, another important soft skill is **time management and work ethic**. The better CMOs I have dealt with understand the importance of time management—they value the time of their partners and their colleagues and are also respectful of maintaining a good work ethic. Since in marketing you do deal with numerous inside and outside partners, you need to ensure that situations are dealt with in a timely manner.

India and Indian consumers are changing rapidly. The way we buy products is changing. Our tastes are changing. To be successful in marketing, one of the most important soft skill is **agility/adaptability/learning**. You have to be able to adapt to the changing market needs, and be ready to learn new skills and new concepts. For instance, CMOs who are in the forty-plus age group have had to learn digital marketing from scratch. Some of the smarter ones have a designated young colleague to do 'reverse mentoring'; here, a young colleague teaches the senior colleague. How ready are you to admit, 'I don't know that, can someone help me understand this?' When you put your ego aside, you will learn a lot more.

Many of the CMOs I spoke with remember their sales stint; how they had excellent managers who taught them all about field sales. In their turn, they remember the way they provided leadership to their sales teams. **Leadership** is the ability to guide and motivate action from a group towards a desired goal. How you can guide and mentor a team? How can you help your team fly higher? As a young marketing executive, you may believe that days of leadership are many years away. You have no one reporting to you. The truth is that even the young brand manager has a team looking at them as leaders; the team could be from the ad or research agency. Your leadership skills can get honed by the way you deal with your external partners as well as your peers. And then, one day, you will get your own team to demonstrate your leadership skills. Remember, a leader leads by example. You cannot expect your team to have good work ethic if you don't have one. You cannot expect your team to have high integrity if you don't demonstrate it. Leadership is also about taking those risks and encouraging your team to do the same by providing them a safety net.

> 'Marketing is anything but bluff. It takes years to hone one's skills.'
>
> —*Amit Doshi, CMO, Lenovo India*

These are but some of the hard and soft skills you need to succeed in marketing. Their emphasis will change depending on your level in the organisation or the industry you are operating in. A skill like negotiation may be more important if you are in a B2B organisation as opposed to a B2C one. Below, I have included a few books, articles and YouTube and podcast links that could be of use to you as you embark on your skill development journey.

Marketing Mixology is an attempt to give young, aspiring executives and entrepreneurs a bird's eye view of the skills needed for marketing success. The core of the book was about four skills: brand building, understanding consumers, negotiations/selling and communications. The soft and hard skills discussed here are additional ingredients to make a great marketing career.

A terrific cocktail calls for good ingredients added in the right proportions and mixed the right way. A marketing career, too, calls for the right mixology of key skills. Good luck!

Additional Resources

1. Rama Bijapurkar, *We Are Like That Only*
2. Ambi Parameswaran, *Sponge: Leadership Lessons I Learnt from My Clients*
3. Ambi Parameswaran, *Nawabs, Nudes, Noodles: India through 50 Years of Advertising*
4. Theodore Levitt, *Marketing Myopia*, Harvard Business Review
5. Gary Zaltman, *How Customers Think*
6. Subroto Sengupta, *Brand Positioning*
7. Peter Drucker, *Practice of Management*
8. Larry Bossidy and Ram Charan, *Execution*
9. Donald Miller, *Building a Story Brand*
10. Seth Godin, *Permission Marketing*
11. Nir Eyal, *Hooked*
12. Prakash Iyer, *Secret of Leadership*
13. R Gopalakrishnan, *Bonsai Manager*
14. Harish Bhat, *The Curious Marketer*
15. K. Ganesh, *Mastering Disruption*
16. Sudhir Sitapati, *The CEO Factory*
17. Jessie Paul, *No Money Marketing*
18. Professor Scott Galloway, NYU (YouTube)

19. BE Positive – Conversations with CMOs (ET BrandEquity, YouTube)
20. HBR IdeaCast (podcast)
21. Adam Grant, Worklife (podcast)
22. Katy Milkman, Choiceology (podcast)

Acknowledgements

Marketing Mixology, as the title says, is a result of mixing many disparate efforts.

It began a few years ago when I was asked to write two mini-books as Amazon Kindle exclusives. The mini-books I wrote on negotiation and brand building did rather well (special thanks to Karthik Venkatesh for his inputs on those). When the rights of the two mini-books came back to me after Amazon's contract concluded, I had the beginning of *Marketing Mixology*. The first two ingredients were in place, though I didn't know it yet.

It was my ever-vigilant literary agent and friend Anish Chandy who suggested that the mini-books, combined with another two, could become a full-fledged book on basic marketing concepts. My thanks to V.K. Karthika and Gautam Padmanabhan of Westland Books, Pratilipi, for green-lighting the project.

As I started working on the book I realized that I had a treasure trove of information about the career journey of chief marketing officers through the series of interviews I had done for ET BrandEquity. Thank you Prasad Sangameshwaran (editor of ETBrandEquity.com) for inviting me to be the host of this BE+ [BE Positive] series. Special thanks to the CMOs, from India and abroad, who graciously took time out to speak with me about their career and learning journey. The videos are all available on ET BrandEquity YouTube channel. To maintain consistency, I have used the titles and company affiliations that they had when they sat down for the interviews with me. My gratitude to Jasneet Bachal, Siddesh Joglekar, Pawan Sarda, Sumit Mathur, Mehul Kapadia, Hitu Chawla, Rajashree R., Ashish Tiwari, Raka Sinha, Anil Viswanathan, Santosh Iyer, Bidisha Nagaraj, Chandramohan Mehra, Shubhranshu Singh, Deepika Warrier, Viju Nair, Anshul Khanna, Siddhartha Butalia, Sapna Arora, Sundar Madakshira, Salil Murthy, Vivek Sharma, Sumit Mathur, Smita Murarka, Deepali Naair, Mayur Hola, Amit Doshi, Harish Narayanan and Virat Kullar for their patience and wisdom.

With the help of Sugam Pagaria, a former colleague at SPJIMR, I managed to extract many wonderful quotes from those twenty-five interviews; some of them are included in the book.

While writing this book it was clear that I did not want to create another 400-page tome on marketing. With the help of Anish and Aurodeep Mukherjee, I honed in on four topics to cover: branding, selling/negotiation, consumer understanding and communications. Aurodeep made me rework all my old content and hence what you have in this book is freshly homogenised 'mixology' content. Properly mixed, so to speak.

The book is meant for a young executive looking for a break in marketing/sales. It would also be useful for an MBA student who is struggling with the aforementioned 400-page marketing tome. How to make the book a light read? A few diagrams and charts, yes. Something more? How about cartoons?

Shobha Prasad graciously gave me permission to use a few cartoons from her book *Funny Business—Consumers, Corporates and Other Cartoons*. Shobha is a highly respected market researcher who has embraced cartooning as a hobby. Her book is a collection of cartoons all inspired by her real-life experience working with consumers and clients.

As we were wondering what title we should adopt for the book, one thing was very clear, we did not want it to sound like yet another serious book on marketing. There are enough out there (some very good ones by my friends). I wanted a light touch in the name of the book but struggled for a few weeks. Everything I suggested was rejected by (take your pick) Anish, Aurodeep or Karthika. It was then that I had started using ChatGPT for some of my branding work. Why not use AI to suggest a title? After much prompting and reprompting, I managed to find this pearl *Marketing Mixology*. Viola, I had my title and fortunately Anish, Aurodeep and Karthika loved it too. Moral of the story: Who says ChatGPT cannot be creative? With the right set of prompts, you can get good ideas from ChatGPT and it is then up to you to pick the one that will work. Thanks to Siddhesh Joglekar for helping me navigate the ChatGPT ecosystem.

Thanks to Sanjana T. for a fine job of editing the final book (raising the right questions from the perspective of a reader, cutting out irrelevant material and more).

Thanks to Saurabh Garge for the excellent cover.

Amrita Talwar of Westland and her team, including Divya Shah, have all been a big help in the marketing of my previous books. I look forward to their continued support. My past books, published by Westland, have had the benefit of publicity support from Moe's Art (Mayank Sen and team). Advance thanks to them for their help with this book.

As the book was getting ready, I reached out to a few friends to go through it and, if deserving, provide it with a few lines as advance praise. Everyone I approached readily agreed. Thanks to Harish Bhat, K. Ganesh, Sudhir Sitapati, Kunal Bahl, Farooq Adam, Jessie Paul, Harshil Karia, Radhika Gupta and Rama Bijapurkar for their kind words.

My wife Nithya reads all that I write and always has a point of view that I truly value. Special thanks to her for her critical inputs.

Finally, this book is here because of the continuous support I have received from readers like you. Not a week goes by without someone messaging me or tagging me on social media about something I've written. Many thanks to all of them. I do hope they will enjoy this book as well and use it to turbo-charge their own career journey in marketing. My best wishes!

Also by Ambi Parameswaran

FCB-ULKA Brand Building Advertising: Concepts and Cases

Understanding Consumers: Building Powerful Brands Through Consumer Research

Building Brand Value: Five Steps to Building Powerful Brands

Ride The Change: A Perspective on the Changing Indian Consumer, Market and Marketing

DRAFTFCB+ULKA Brand Building Advertising: Concepts and Cases (Book II) (with Kinjal Medh)

Strategic Brand Management (with Kevin Lane Keller, Vanitha Swaminathan and Isaac Jacob)

For God's Sake: An Adman on the Business of Religion

Nawabs, Nudes, Noodles: India Through 50 Years of Advertising

Sponge: Leadership Lessons I Learnt From My Clients

Spring: Bouncing Back From Rejection

All The World's a Stage: A Personal Branding Story